HAROLD A. COVINGTON

THE MARCH UP COUNTRY

1987
Liberty Bell Publications
Reedy WV

First edition published 1987 by
Liberty Bell Publications
Reedy, WV USA

Reprinted 2004 by
Liberty Bell Publications
PO Box 890
York, SC 29745
www.libertybellpublications.com

ISBN: 1-59364-009-9

Printed in the United States of America

HAROLD A. COVINGTON was born in Burlington, North Carolina on September 14th, 1953. During his teenaged years he received a number of minor awards for achievement in creative writing, music, and the dramatic arts. He attended the Governor's School of North Carolina in 1970 in drama. He worked as a cub reporter for the local newspaper in Chapel Hill, N.C., and his weekly columns became the paper's most popular Sunday feature, despite their frequent attacks on the behavior of black students at the high school in Chapel Hill.

Covington's political career began in the United States Army in 1972, when he joined a National Socialist front group called the White Servicemen's League and was expelled from the service for racial agitation. He joined the national headquarters staff of the National Socialist White People's Party (NSWPP) in Arlington, Virginia and shortly thereafter became editor of the party newspaper, *White Power.* After a year as editor he resigned and emigrated to Southern Africa, where he worked for a short time for a civil engineering firm in Johannesburg before going north to enlist in the Rhodesian Army, where he participated in the defense of the country against black terrorists. While in the military he assisted local Whites in the formation of the Rhodesia White People's Party (RWPP). The party was suppressed by the Ian Smith government and Covington was arrested on a charge of allegedly "terrorizing Jews." He was deported in 1976, along with two other American National Socialists who had been politically active. Two years later the Smith regime surrendered to the blacks and in 1980 Rhodesia became a Marxist dictatorship appropriately renamed "Zimbabwe" after some local ruins.

Returning to his native North Carolina, Covington formed a local National Socialist group and wrote articles and books for White Power Publications, Samisdat Publishers in Canada, the newspaper *New Order,* and other periodicals. He edited and published his own newsletter, *White Carolina,* as well as a short-lived theoretical journal, the *National Socialist Review.* He also ran in four North Carolina elections over as many years, gaining 34% of the White vote in a State Senate campaign in 1978 and a whopping 43%, representing 56,000 votes, in the 1980 Republican primary for State Attorney General. He assisted in the defense campaign for the "Greensboro 16" in 1980, and in 1979 was elected Party Leader of the National Socialist Party of America (NSPA) by a special conference of officers.

In December 1980 the Federal government began a full-scale offensive against the NSPA, utilizing legal frame-ups and informers inside the organization as well as financial pressure. Despite Covington's best efforts, the organization collapsed. In September of 1981 he was ordered to leave the country or be killed by Federal agents seeking to suppress his testimony in a new round of Greensboro trials. In March of 1982 he was again told point-blank to leave or be murdered. He spent the next five years in South Africa, Great Britain, and Ireland, constantly being "moved on" by the authorities. In April of 1987 he returned to the United States in defiance of the Federal threats. To date there has been no retaliation from the government.

Covington has been married twice, both marriages ending in divorce. He has one son and one daughter in Ireland who are presently legally barred from the United States.

In 1980 he published his only major work of fiction, an historical novel set in Medieval England entitled *Rose of Honor.* The book was suppressed by the Jews, who bought out the entire press run from the publisher and destroyed it so that only a few copies survive.

TABLE OF CONTENTS

This book is for Fred, my fellow "squalid pamphleteer," in memory of 30 January 1976 and in commemoration of that land of hope and glory which was Rhodesia.

INTRODUCTION

This book is written for the practical and ideological instruction of revolutionaries. Its primary purpose is to increase the effectiveness and influence of the worldwide White, Aryan resistance movement. It does not pretend to be any kind of complete analysis of the present racial geopolitical situation, nor does it pretend to be aimed at the mass of White people in general. Readers will find much left unsaid here, but if they are the type of person I am trying to reach they will be able to fill in the gaps themselves.

This book is based on certain fundamental principles, and it is essential that the reader be more or less in agreement with these principles before he begins. They are:

1.) The White, Aryan race is in imminent danger of physical extinction through subversion, miscegenation, and outright violence from non-Whites. If present trends continue, within another fifty years we will have passed the point of no return.

2.) The second and most crucial basic premise of this book is that even this late in the day, *it is still possible to reverse this decline,* and to re-assert White authority over the globe.

3.) It is vitally necessary for the good of all life on this planet that this be done. Over the past thirty years the lesser races have proven themselves incapable of self-government, incompetent to manage their own economies, unable to maintain order internally or sustain peace externally, and, in short, have demonstrated that they constitute a threat to the whole world environment and all terrestrial life.

4.) The malevolent activities of the Jewish race have a good deal to do with the decline of the White man and his culture.

5.) This having been said, the primary responsibility for what has happened to our people rests not upon the Jews or on any outside force, but within ourselves, because of our childish inability to come to terms with reality and with the magnitude of our own racial destiny. The prerequisite for White victory is a spiritual transformation of our race from within.

6.) The only method by which White victory may be attained is through a series of revolutions in every White or partially White country, wherein White racial nationalists assume state power and then proceed to carry out a complete transmutation of the societies in which these revolutions take place.

If you have difficulty with any of these precepts, then I will tell you quite frankly that you are not yet ready to read this book. Instead, return to the source from which you obtained it. More than likely, that same source will be able to provide you with a complete course of basic ideological instruction and background material for in-depth study on the problems of Zionism and Jewry, Communism, international finance, liberalism, multi-racialism, and the way in which all of these interlink. Do not attempt to read *The March Up Country* until you are mentally and morally prepared. Otherwise you will be wasting both your time and mine.

I need to give those of you who are already committed to White revolution a brief explanation about the book and its contents. *The March Up Country* is intended to prepare your mind and your heart for the terrible period in your life which is approaching. I am not going to go into a long and detailed recital of all the obstacles and ordeals which await you. You probably already know, if you don't you'll soon find out, and in any case no words of mine printed on this sheet of paper can adequately prepare you to face it all. That strength you will find within yourselves when the time comes. Don't worry, it won't fail you. The spirit of our race is strong and in the blood of every man and woman of us, nor are a few short decades of boob-tube and Big Macs sufficient to drain it from our genes. The iron will and the lion's courage of our forefathers will be there in your own soul when you need them.

But while the spirit is strong, you will find that the flesh is mortal and weak. Let me be blunt: the revolutionary period of your life, however long or short it may turn out to be, is going to be the worst thing that ever happened to you. This struggle destroys people. It uses them, drains them, then tosses them aside. The sheer massive amount of work, time, money, and concentration which you will have to invest in order to gain one paltry, agonizing inch of progress will break your heart. The purpose of this book is to make sure that you *do it right,* and that we all keep that bitterly contested and brutally won inch of progress which you will achieve. My brothers, I am sick and tired of this movement getting nowhere. I am sick and tired of time, effort, money, and sometimes blood being blown away to no end. I am revolted and angry at the spectacle of brave young men and women going to prison for forty and sixty years for *nothing.* I am fed up with the constant dead ends, the "Great White Hopes" who turn out to be thieves, government spies, or *non compos mentis.* I am weary unto death of seeing youth, hope, idealism, and enthusiasm seized, diverted, leeched off, and then crushed by psychopolitical swindlers who view this sacred cause as a business which provides them with a comfortable living, and who have no intention of ever doing anything seriously to incommode the enemy.

This movement has been simply drifting for years, with no direction or central guidance, no coordination, no effort to prevent waste and duplication of effort, and without the foggiest notion of where we are headed. That must end. I claim no magical, quasi-papal infallibility. If you question anything I say in this book, then come up with your own answers and see if they make more sense in your own situation. We need to get into the habit of using our heads for something besides hatracks. One of the main advantages which the White revolutionary has over the enemy, if he is sharp enough to use it, is the ability to think faster and to implement decisions much quicker than the cumbersome, senile bureaucracy we are confronting. We can run rings around Uncle Slime if we'll just put our minds to it. I hope I can give you all some ideas in these pages, but don't think of this book as some kind of Bible. Set your goal, work like hell for it, follow your instincts, and above all, *think.* And we'll beat the scoundrels,

The March Up Country is written from an American viewpoint. Since I am an American Southerner, it makes sense for me to address the tactical situation I am most familiar with. However, most of what I say here is true of all Zionist Occupational Governments (ZOGs) throughout the Western world. All ZOGs in so-called "democracies" use more or less the same scam — *panem et circenses,* boob tube mind control, love-thy-nigger brainwashing, letting the White peasantry elect a few windbags to a legislative talking shop, etc. We need to recover the United States or a part thereof as well as Canada, Australia, New Zealand, and Western Europe, although a few countries there such as Ireland and Germany pose special problems. It would be nice to hang onto South Africa as well, although right now I'm not too sanguine about their chances. At present it seems likely that by the time a White racial nationalist revolution does occur in some country which would then be in a position to help South Africa, the country will have been overrun with the assistance of a bribed National Party régime in

Pretoria. That's another five million Whites down the tube because we have been wasting our time on yellow-belly games.

This book does not contain all the answers, but it does tell you what questions you should be asking as a White revolutionary. We are entering a crucial period because under the best of circumstances the culmination of a successful revolution is going to take a span of years measurable well into two figures, and if we don't get our act together and make a serious beginning very soon the clock is going to run out. I am convinced that we can still pull it off, despite the decades we have wasted on assorted silliness. We can still pull it off if we *can stop the nonsense* and get *started NOW.* The preliminaries have lasted overlong but now they are over. It's time for the main event.

Also by Harold A. Covington:

Bonnie Blue Murder: A Civil War Murder Mystery

Fire and Rain

Other Voices, Darker Rooms: Eight Grim Tales

Revelation 9

Rose of Honor

Slow Coming Dark: A Novel of the Age of Clinton

The Black Flame

The Hill of the Ravens

The Renegade

The Stars in Their Path: A Novel of Reincarnation

Vindictus: A Novel of History's First Gunfighter

I.
THE PRESENT SITUATION

Because of the fluid nature of the current racial and geopolitical situation, I can only give you a very broad, general discussion here. Bear in mind that I am writing in the summer of 1987 and future events may either confirm or invalidate much of what I say here. Nonetheless, the best place to start is always at the beginning.

Politically and demographically, the White race is in full flight across the world. Whites now comprise only 15% of the global population, and that small fraction is rapidly aging. Every year the White birthrate drops, the non-White birthrate skyrockets, and the median age of the few remaining Whites rises. Things have gotten so bad in some European countries, such as France and Holland, that the governments there are openly begging White couples to have more children and are offering tax breaks and financial incentives for them to do so. The inundation of the White population in the United States has become so obvious to the man in the street that a few mentions of the problem have even leaked into the System media. In Canada, the vile Zionist Occupational Government in Ottawa has actually exhibited the sheer gall to use the declining White birthrate as an excuse to import non-White Asian immigrants on grounds of "underpopulation"!

The one bright spot in the unrelieved gloom is the Republic of Ireland, the only White nation on the face of the earth which is presently reproducing itself and actually increasing its numbers. An incredible 60% of the Irish are under age 25. The complete dearth of employment in the Republic has led to a massive outflow of emigration, mostly of young and well-educated White men and women who go to America, Canada, Australia, New Zealand, South Africa, and the EEC countries in search of jobs. Right now there are an estimated 80,000 to 100,000 young Irish immigrants in the United States alone. All these young Seans and Bridgets are a welcome shot in the arm to the White gene pools in all these countries.

But in America the influx of Irish is a drop in the bucket compared to the tidal wave of non-Whites from Latin America, the Caribbean,

Asia, and Africa. In growing portions of the United States the English language is being pushed out and replaced by Spanish or Chinese. Even as I write these words, hordes of non-Whites are lining up at government offices all over the country to take advantage of the insane "amnesty" which the System has offered them. The high-tech boom has apparently increased the need for cheap, non-unionized labor at minimum wage or below to the point where the System is even willing to risk the wrath of the once politically omnipotent negroids in order to secure its supply of cut-price workers. (One of the more edifying experiences for today's White racial nationalist in this country is to watch the niggers squabble with the Hispanics, the Chinese, the South Koreans, and other "new Democrats" who are elbowing the blacks aside from the trough whereat the bubble-lips have so long slurped.)

In fact, America is well on the way towards becoming a polyglot, multi-lingual, multi-racial collage similar to the old Austro-Hungarian empire. Those of my readers who are National Socialists will recall the Leader Adolf Hitler's comments on multi-racial empires in general and the Hapsburg state in particular. The inevitable fate of all such hybrids is to be broken down into the component parts. Yeats put it well: "Things fall apart; the center cannot hold." In this gradual breakdown of the American empire, I believe, lies the hope of the White race.

Revolutions never take place in strong, confident, vigorous and expanding societies. They take place in societies which are spiritually demoralized and confused, in cultures which have lost their sense of direction and purpose, in states which are gripped by indecision and filled with self-doubt, among peoples who question their own entitlement to what their destiny has achieved. This situation now exists in America, nor is this likely to change. Add a burgeoning, brawling population of a dozen different minority groups and a dozen more financial and political special interest groups, and you have a society that is ready to go prompt critical and disassemble. America today is ripe for a movement, any movement, which offers the vision, the clear-cut plan, and the sense of purpose which the System has lost. There is no God-given eternal law making the North American continent and its inhabitants immune from the laws of human nature and *realpolitik.* We MUST ensure that, as far as the White Americans are concerned, it is the racial nationalist resistance that commandeers their allegiance and not some weirdo lefty cult.

Comprehension: Jewish control of the media and other power sources is getting weaker and will continue to do so.

This is not to say that the power of the Jews' money and of their media are not still formidable indeed. But the slippage is definitely there, and it is detectable on a year to year basis. There has always been a tendency in the Movement to credit these creatures with nearly supernatural powers and abilities. Their power is real enough, and will remain lethal for years, but bear in mind that like everything else Yehudi has, it is a borrowed power. The power of the Jews to hurt our people comes through the insidious combination of money and mind control which they have mastered over the centuries. It's a deadly trick, right enough, but in the final analysis I am convinced that they will not be able to keep it up indefinitely. Our minds are first-rate, and for all their cleverness the minds of the Jews are really only second or third rate. Eventually they're going to lose control, like the Wizard of Oz when the little dog pulled aside the curtain concealing the charlatan and apparatus behind all the smoke and noise. It's all done with mirrors, after all, and one day the mirrors will shatter.

Today I see outright criticism and condemnation of Israel in the press and even in the electronic media, which would have been absolutely unthinkable back when I first got into alternative politics fifteen years ago. I pick up publications such as *National Lampoon* and I read savage satires on the Jews, which would never have seen the light of day a few years ago. I see System politicians suddenly changing horses in midstream and angling after Arab money and Arab influence instead of the traditional Zionist cornucopia of goodies. The fact that much of this anti-Zionist criticism and caricature comes from the Left is irrelevant; the fact that it exists at all is what is significant. The Jews, for all their power, haven't been able to stop the Arabs, the true Semites, from competing at the same game, and now the Arab Semites are starting to beat them at it. True, the White resistance doesn't have Arab money or a string of governments in power, but it does show that Yehudi is far from invincible.

Another exciting turn of events we White racial nationalists can look forward to in the coming years is the crumble and collapse of the "Holocaust" canard. Right now, we are being inundated with another wave of "Holocaust" garbage — TV specials, memorials, speeches by *shabbaz-goy* politicians, the shameful deportation of elderly Eastern Europeans to torture and ritual murder behind the Iron Curtain or in the nauseating Zionist state of Israel. And yet, as nearly as I can determine, it's just rolling off people's backs. Not that they doubt it happened, since revisionist material is by no means able to compete with the Jewish media on a mass scale. The majority of White Americans accept that the alleged killing of six million Jews took place, in the same way that they accept that Columbus discovered America in 1492 and George Washington chopped down the cherry tree. (In actual fact, of course, these last two historical "facts" are as false as the Holocaust lie.) They accept the six million story in the same casual manner, but *they just don't care.*

It is this the Jews can't seem to grasp. They spend countless millions of dollars every year perpetuating a mythical event that never happened, and considering the power at their command, naturally enough they are able to achieve a 99% belief rate among the people they want to deceive. Their error lies in the whole basic premise that what may or may not have happened fifty years ago matters. It doesn't. I spoke to a 20-year-old girl the other day about the "Holocaust." At first she didn't know what I meant. When I explained it to her she said, "Oh, yeah, that," and then changed the subject to her forthcoming trip to the beach with her boyfriend over the long Memorial Day weekend — a holiday, ironically enough, intended to commemorate our ancestors who died fighting the Jews' wars against Europe for them. My 20-year-old didn't think that way, either. All the veterans she's ever known fought against the Communists.

Those millions of dollars the Jews spend on "Holocaust" drivel are showing less and less return every year. Revisionist history is making strides despite the ADL's suppression and the JDL's bombs and murder. In another ten or fifteen years the supply of elderly Croatians and Lithuanians is going to run out, unless the Jews can convince people that the *SS* enlisted ten-year-olds. Also dying out will be the gaggle of screaming Hebes who wave their tattooed arms and rave about gas chambers, although I imagine that with Mosaic ingenuity the supply of these creatures will be stretched to the absolute limits of goy credulity. However, I suspect that long before the last "survivor" finally croaks the tissue of the great lie will have worn so thin that even the most headstrong of Zionists will recognize the inutility of keeping it up. Basically, we're all entering a new phase now, both we and the enemy. In the world of Star Wars, grainy black and white photo fakes and scratchy newsreel film just can't compete with holograms and laser discs in grabbing the attention of *boobus Americanus.* In a few years the Jews will, for all practical purposes, be minus one of their primary weapons against us. Not before time.

The Senile System

Right now there is only one thing holding American society together, and that is the almighty dollar. When that goes, the breakup of the North American continent into fragments will follow soon after. Watch the deficit, my brothers, it is the time bomb that will eventually blow our enemies apart. When that happens we must be ready to pick up the pieces. It won't happen any time at all soon, because this continent is still huge and rich and incredibly resilient despite decades of abuse, but it will happen eventually.

Money is the only cement which binds all the disparate elements in America together. True enough, it is a powerful cohesive force. It makes things happen, gets things done. It buys the sullen quiescence of the violent non-White minorities and keeps them more or less tractable in their ghettos. God knows, money buys our own people by the truck-load: police officers, Federal agents and bureaucrats, district attorneys, judges, media reporters and controllers, the professional liars of the press, lawyers by the thousand, and the legislators who make the laws, the loathsome Yuppies who keep the computers whirring and the creaky old machinery greased — they all do it for that almighty green-back. As Dr. Revilo Oliver once said in a letter to a friend of mine, "....they are completely unable to distinguish between the cool riffle of a stack of hundred-dollar bills and the Voice of God."

Comprehension: The people who make the actual decisions in American society fall into three categories. They are all either criminals, certifiably insane, or both.

It is absolutely essential for all White revolutionaries to understand that the people who rule us are totally unfit to do so, and that the most vital element in the successful consolidation of the revolution once it is achieved will be a 100% replacement of all upper-echelon personnel, in everything. This by no means includes "elected" officials only. Indeed, the vast bulk of actual decision-making today is carried out by people who are unelected and whose existence is only faintly suspected by the population they control.

Every White or partially White nation has its own clique of loosely-knit individuals and groups who actually make policy, implement decisions, set trends, manipulate the information which is, allowed to reach the White population, and, in short, do the actual running of things. 1 don't like the term "ruling class" myself. Not only is it Marxist but it is also far too pat. The actual reality isn't that simple. The various upper-crud cliques are often overlapping in membership, working at cross purposes, sometimes mutually antagonistic, and seldom have any clear idea of the big picture or even of their own role in things. "Class" implies a distinctive identity, a hierarchical pecking order, at least some hereditary clement, and very few of these exist in America today. The best analogy I can draw is that America is one big garbage heap, and certain individuals and groups have clawed their way to a higher level where the smell is a bit less intense and they can help themselves to the more tasty morsels of offal. The bulk of us peons, of course, is buried under the heap, down here with the coffee grounds and the tin cans and the moldy hamburger.

Nonetheless, an identifiable ruling élite which monopolizes money and power does in fact exist. Once you as a White revolutionary understand that these people are, in fact, without exception criminals and lunatics, then all of a sudden a lot that was previously incomprehensible will become clear. Base your revolutionary thought and your tactics on this knowledge, and already you've got one important edge over them right from the beginning.

The criminal element among our upper crud are blatant and obvious. They regularly trip over their own laws which were designed to keep the peasantry down, and end up getting hauled into courtrooms and slammers with their coats over their heads. Presidents, Cabinet members, Senators, Congressmen, senior intelligence officials, top civil servants, state governors and bureaucrats, cops from Commissioner on down to patrolman, judges, district attorneys, tax officials, contractors, businessmen, mayors and aldermen, corporate executives, Hollywood producers and stars, you name them. Every week the greedy pigs get caught with their fingers in the cookie jar. We see them exposed, indicted, grilled by grand juries, fined, plea-bargaining, negotiating for immunity through their high-powered lawyers to rat on their partners in crime, fleeing the country, blowing their brains out at televised press conferences. Very seldom do the repulsive maggots have the guts to take the consequences of their own vileness, and very seldom are they required to.

Every crime, every sin, every abomination in the book is rampant among our masters and mistresses. Our rulers snort, ingest, or inject every known drug into their bodies. They indulge in every known sexual aberration and have invented some new perversions which would startle the most depraved Roman emperor. They regularly appear in public or on TV bagged on cocaine, strung out on pills, or just plain drunk. The women of our ruling élite regularly murder their own children through abortion. Both sexes periodically maim or kill the odd peasant through drunken or drug-crazed behavior with cars, aircraft, guns, power speedboats, or general idiotic horseplay. They then proceed, almost without exception, to buy their way out of trouble with aplomb. The one bright spot is that many of the disgusting swine are dropping dead from drug overdoses or rotting away into loathsome putrescence like M. Valdemar from AIDS.

I won't discuss the breathtaking hypocrisy involved in all this because words simply fail me. But I will say a few words about the one hobby, the one vocation, the one *raison d'être* that our ruling élite pursue above all others.

They *steal.* Great God Almighty, does our massas in de big house steal! Attila the Hun's hordes were street corner shoplifters compared to the legions of thieves and parasites who loot America's riches from their plush offices and penthouses. Our lords and masters steal through every known form of fraud. They falsify accounts, cook books, dummy up their tax returns, take kickbacks and bribes from organized crime, accept bogus "consultation fees" from multinational corporations in exchange for corrupt favors. They engage in every conceivable form of embezzlement and defalcation.

They steal in goods and services. They take junkets to the Bahamas and the French Riviera on phony "government business". They steal gasoline, meals, hotel accommodation, night club entertainment, fees for straight and homosexual prostitutes, liquor, clothing, and write it all off to the taxpayers. They steal government equipment, vehicles from motor pools, computer software, office supplies, military weapons and rations, and re-sell it all on the black market. Police regularly sell confiscated drugs back to the same criminals they got it from, or else use the drugs themselves. Top civil servants buy drugs with taxpayers' money and Wall Street stockbrokers trade in cocaine like any other commodity. Judges sell justice to the highest bidder, governors and parole boards sell freedom to vicious hoodlums and killers. Bureaucrats steal millions of dollars every year through computer fraud, postal niggers steal mail, and everybody steals from petty cash.

The one motivation for a large percentage of our politicians, civil servants, and other upper crud is to get at the public trough so that they can steal. It's that damned simple, pure naked greed. Most of them are cunning enough to realize that a certain minimum level of outward decorum must be maintained, but periodically their all-consuming greed gets the better of them. Throwing caution to the winds, they leap headlong into the trough of wealth that White America produces, wallowing in all that lovely money and squealing in animalistic delight like the swine they are. So loudly do they wallow and squeal that they disturb the other hogs who have been slurping more quietly, and so the renegades must be indicted for misbehaving themselves. Some of them even end up doing a little time in one of the régime's luxury prison camps for "white collar" offenders, complete with golf course, Olympic length swimming pool, and aerobics for weight-watchers.

White revolutionaries should bear in mind that as reprehensible as these greedy mugs are, they are more or less sane and they therefore constitute the greatest actual threat to the movement. *It is the criminal element in the upper classes which will come down on us the hardest.* This is because they instinctively sense a threat to their incomes. Any White activist who has ever tangled with the System will affirm that the main muscle is always provided, not by Jews or even by non-Whites who are difficult to discipline and control, but by White mercenaries who attack their own people's revolutionary vanguard in exchange for a monthly check giving them a tiny fraction of the wealth that the Establishment loots from their race. So far, these mercenaries have remained more or less loyal, although, to be honest, so far there has been little risk to them in arresting and framing White political activists. We generally surrender peacefully like little lambs and get hauled off into living hell screaming "You can't *do* this to me", quite oblivious to the fact that the System *can* do it and *is* doing it to us.

How loyal the police and the other mercenary enforcers will remain to their paymasters once taking on White revolutionaries becomes hazardous to their health will be difficult to say. Look hard enough and eventually one can find somebody or other who is willing to do anything for money, and I imagine that right up to the end there will be a few Whites who will be willing to serve the Jews for increasingly huge salaries in worthless Federal Reserve notes.

The insane element in our ruling élite is a bit harder to quantify. I used to call them the techno-bureaucracy, but the media have obliged me by thinking of an apt nomenclature for these loathsome people, "Yuppies." When I say that they are insane, I do not mean that all Yuppies wear tricorn hats and believe they are Napoleon, although many of them do suffer nervous breakdowns during the course of their careers and become actual rubber-room material. The madness I refer to is a peculiar form of schizophrenia, a divorcement from reality. Yuppies eventually reach a stage where they are incapable of distinguishing between reality and their own high-tech fantasies. They begin to ignore the evidence of their own observations, their own deductions, their own senses, and instead decide that the contents of their computer print-outs are the reality. The world of the Yuppie is a completely artificial one, and they become so absorbed in it that the higher they get promoted into the upper-crud strata the more they cut themselves loose from planet Earth as the vast majority of humanity must experience it.

There are certain entrance qualifications for Yuppie-dom. First off, a true Yuppie is a drone. He is an advertising executive, a marketing or sales director, any kind of computer hacker other than a scientific one, a systems analyst or database specialist, a stockbroker or invest-ment analyst, an economist, a government bureaucrat, a "managerial" whosis, or the Yuppie profession *par excellence,* a lawyer. In other words, *the Yuppie produces nothing.* He provides no essential service such as a doctor or medical technician. He manufactures nothing, unlike the civil engineer or the production manager. The Yuppie simply manipulates paper, money, and information, for which he is paid a grossly inflated salary five or ten times that of the productive White worker who actually does society's genuine labor.

Secondly, a true Yuppie prefers to deal with paper rather than with people. His one obsessive fear is of being forced to confront and communicate with actual, living human beings rather than with machines or written directives. The Yuppie world has developed a whole new jargon of non-communication, the purpose of which is to program themselves like they program their computers to respond to human situations, when they are forced to confront them, as a computer responds to "input". Most will be familiar with this type of programmed gibberish. It is a terminology designed, like Orwell's Newspeak, to convey as *little* genuine information or idea content as possible. "Interface", "hands-on", "state of the art", "on-line", "high tech, high spec", "let's do lunch", "he gives great meeting", etc. The Song of the Jabberwock on floppy disks.

The Yuppies are the shock troops of mediocrity militant. It is they who keep the paper flowing, the computers whirring, the welfare checks rolling off the printers, and the wheels of the decrepit, crumbling System machine greased and patched up. Yuppies have come face to face with their own mediocrity and lack of moral fiber, accepted it, and systematized it. They are the ultimate materialists, measuring status and success in terms of money, perks, and high-tech gimcrack toys. Devoid of principles or spiritual concepts, they become wrapped up in their print-outs and cocooned in their indirect-light, bland, carpeted, ionized-air environment. When they bother to look out upon the real world where most of us must live and toil and survive, they are generally looking down, from high within a monolithic office block of glass and concrete and steel, or from their plush climate-controlled, security fenced condos. Like Alice, they eventually become able to believe six impossible things before breakfast.

Herein lies the principal weakness of the Yuppie managerial class, the one which we can exploit to achieve their destruction. Unable to distinguish between reality and the illusions they themselves create to sustain their own fantasy world, they fall into the fatal trap of *actually believing the nonsense which the System puts out to confuse and fragment the White working population.* Liberalism, racial equality, feminism and other sexual perversions, the myth of the entrepreneur, the myth of democracy, all of these are meant to anesthetize the productive White workers and stop them from organizing politically and still keep them working all the while. In point of fact, this barrage of psychopolitical offal pretty much fails. Very few White workers today actually believe System propaganda about equality, because it contradicts common sense and it is at variance with what they see every day with their own eyes. Whites haven't organized politically yet because there has been no serious White political movement, a subject we will address at some length later on in this book. But meanwhile, in their clean and luxurious plasti-steel towers high above the common herd, the Yups have come to actually believe all this equality and freedom garbage.

The received wisdom states that negroids are equal to Whites. So why not give an important assignment to a nigger, then? When the coon flubs it the Yuppie will study the VDU intensely, trying to figure out what went wrong. The received wisdom is that Jews are brilliant geniuses and wonderfully compassionate human beings and just plain better than anybody else. At any rate, that's what they learn in their "sensitivity training" and Holocaust seminars. So when Dr. Shlepstein the analyst tells them in group therapy that they must liberate themselves sexually, then by all means limber up those libidos and all the other moving parts! Pity about all those ex-Yups rotting away in the AIDS ward.

Education is the panacea for all social ills? Come, then, let us educate! Integrate those schools! March those teens into race relations seminars and Holocaust indoctrination classes, and we'll "educate" every racist and anti-Semitic thought right out of their heads!

What do you mean, it's not working? What do you mean, White teenagers today are more racist than ever before in the country's history? That's not what it says right here on page 14 of the print-out! No, there's no discontent among White workers due to affirmative action. This graph right here proves it. White people will never vote for racist candidates in any significant numbers. Those election figures must be a computer error, we'll de-bug it. What White protest? What White rioting? If we didn't see it on the ten o'clock news, it didn't happen. What revolution? There is nothing in our annual projections about any revolution. What are you men in smelly jeans and work clothes doing in here? This area is supposed to be bio-clean so dust particles don't short out our micro-chips. What are you nasty-ass honkies doing with that noose?

Perhaps this is a confession I shouldn't make, but when I was on the run in Europe in 1983 I took a computer course myself. I learned one interesting bit of hacker jargon — "GIGO", which means "garbage in, garbage out." You may think the preceding paragraphs were an exaggeration, and I suppose they are a bit hyperbolic, but you will find that when the revolution is well under way, a huge number of the enemy Yuppie managerial class *simply will not believe it is happening!* Their computers won't tell them so, and they won't take their noses out of their VDUs long enough to look out their own windows into the streets below. Their computers — the computers upon which the régime and the whole System now rely — will tell them nothing of the revolution because no one will have programmed the data banks with the correct input. The other day I saw a little sign over a computer hacker's desk: "We are drowning in a sea of information and yet starving for a few crumbs of knowledge." Posterity will record this as the epitaph of the Yuppie and the System he serves.

The Movement

You now have a brief, very incomplete thumbnail sketch of the 5% of the White population who will be opposing us. What of the nucleus upon which we will build our own 5% which will fight on our side? What shape is the White racial resistance movement in?

All in all, in passably good shape. Quite frankly, it is in better shape than we have any right to expect, considering all the years we have wasted on fools and incompetents and thieves. In the United States we are still able to operate legally, although the parameters of what constitutes "legality" for White racial nationalists are narrowed every year as the Jews use their lackeys in assorted state legislatures to slice away our rights piece by piece, in what they refer to themselves as "salami tactics."

A few of our better leaders have been picked off by Mickey Mouse prosecutions, perjured testimony, and fabricated evidence. As I write, fifteen men are awaiting trial on charges of sedition and assorted other raps as a result of "Operation Clean Sweep," the first Federal offensive aimed openly and blatantly at suppressing dissent from the racial right. A greater problem still is burnout. There are hundreds of first-class leaders out there throughout America who came into racial politics during the 1960s and 1970s, fought for a while, and then left in a state of complete disgust and revulsion at the wretched incompetence, shameless money-grubbing and embezzlement, and revelations of perversion and agent provocateur-ism, which were endemic among the leadership of so many organizations of that time. Finding these men and women, re-charging their spiritual batteries, re-motivating and reactivating them is going to be a major challenge of the future for the Movement as a whole.

A few of the old con men from the '60s and '70s are still around, running their mail-order empires and fleecing the suckers, but increasingly they are being recognized as irrelevant and I believe they will eventually wither away. Some of them have retired to large woodland tracts in the countryside, from which they periodically issue fund appeals more out of old habit than anything else. Most of these sleazy old sinners have given up any pretense of serious political activity and their whole rap has become either a blatant Amway-style rip-off or else they've degenerated into a bizarre mysticism, talking to the trees and babbling about the ancient Aryan gods, which is an irrelevance if not blasphemy. Wotan would have thrown most of these hucksters to the Great Worm had they dared to show their faces among the Aesir. But I digress.

There is still a very considerable and (to me) largely inexplicable reluctance among otherwise serious White activists to confront the whole issue of Movement con men and what is to be done about them. For example, I am personally familiar with one individual who has arguably done more permanent damage to the Movement than any other single person, and who has certainly sabotaged the orthodox National Socialist wing of the Movement beyond all hope of recovery. I personally believe that a digression on this individual's long and shady career would be of value in this section of *The March Up Country. I* would dearly love to name names, give dates, tell where the bodies are buried, and cite chapter and verse as to why this man and all his works should be avoided as things unclean. If nothing else, I might succeed in diverting some of the tens of thousands of dollars this man's devotees pour into his cult every year towards some kind of bona fide racial nationalist activity.

And yet, I can't do so. Why? The answer is simple, and it cuts right to the heart of possibly the biggest internal problem the Resistance faces. For obvious reasons, when you look on the title page of *The March Up Country you* will not find the imprint of a major New York or Boston publishing house. The publishing industry in this country is controlled lock, stock, and barrel by Jews who would cut off their own goolies before they would print and distribute this book, no matter how much money they thought they could make. You will find that this book has been printed by one of the small, peripheral publishing companies who specialize in our kind of material. These companies perform an utterly invaluable service to the Movement, a service literally beyond price. They operate on financial shoestrings and you could hide their profit margins behind a straw. The confidence tricksters whom I would love to expose in these pages all have cash reserves which are, for the Movement, comparatively large. They issue publications which reach many thousands of activists and supporters. They appear on the same platforms as some of the publishers to whom this book will be submitted. In short, they control that crucial fraction of potential sales and distribution that the racial right publishers must have access to in order to survive.

Most of the publishers to whom I refer know that these phony "leaders" are crooks. Many of them have been burned in attempting to do business with them, And yet, a "don't rock the boat" attitude prevails. The publishers cannot afford to muddy the well from which they themselves must draw water. And so the swindlers and thieves and possible government spies, the so-called "racist leaders" who are being blackmailed by the ADL because of tainted ancestry or sexual perversion, the incompetent and greedy and alcoholic generalissimos who have gotten off light so often in the past, will get off light again in this book. They will not be named, their specific crimes and idiocies will not be exposed, and their faulty policies and mediocrity will not be publicly dissected. If I attempted to do so, the publisher who eventually does us all the service of printing and issuing *The March Up Country* will simply exercise his editorial prerogative and excise all reference to them.

I do not blame him for this. From his point of view he would be correct to impose such censorship. He can't afford to muddy the well from which he draws the water he must drink to survive. So he must pay that tribute of silence to men who are responsible for thirty years of failure. Thus his publishing company will survive. Whether the White race will survive is another matter. I am going to lay another comprehension on you now, and if you absorb nothing else in this book, please absorb this:

Comprehension: The White man is, and always has been, his own worst enemy. The Struggle, the Kampf is and always will be a battle against all that is mean-spirited, weak and corrupt within ourselves.

The Jews are not the problem. Strip them of the strength of their hosts and like all parasites they are helpless. The Jews are cockroaches and can be crushed effortlessly once we get our own act together. The Communists are not the problem. Adolf Hitler took about three weeks to clean up Germany from top to bottom. The negroids are not the problem, They are animals and without Jewish or White renegade leadership they can be corralled, albeit with some difficulty due to their savage nature. All of these enemies have done what they have done to us *because we have let them do it.*

Do you want to see the enemy, my brothers? Take a good long look in the mirror. There he is, the man you've got to beat for our race to survive. Everything in this man that is lazy, everything in this man that longs for the easy road and the soft option, everything in his soul that craves the exotic and unusual, everything in his mind that argues for compromise with the forces of darkness and moderation in the pursuit of right — all this you must burn from him with the white-hot fire of rage, the rage of our ancient race, the *furor Teutonicus* that the priests of the insipid new religion used to pray to their Jewish god to deliver them from. Nurse that rage, feed it, temper it, and yet never let it take you over. Like everything else, your rage is a tool, an acetylene torch that can get the job done but which can also blow up in your face if you are careless.

Never be easy with yourself as a revolutionary. Never tolerate sloppiness, indecision, cowardice, or venality — and *never tolerate it in others who profess the White creed.* In your career as an activist you will meet the men (and a few women) of whom I have spoken in the preceding pages. You will be able to detect the odor of male bovine excremental matter that wafts from their direction. You will meet otherwise sincere comrades who say, "Well, yes, so-and-so has his faults, but he's doing *some* good for the cause." This is horse manure. Thieves, renegades, incompetents and drunkards *never* do our cause any good. They blow off good people who take a look at what they're expected to work with and say good-bye. They waste time. They waste money. They lose us ground that other genuine activists have won with their blood, sweat, and tears. Exposing these people and removing them from political activism is one of the prime duties of every White revolutionary.

You will, inevitably, be accused of "spreading disunity", "sowing discord". etc. The difference between legitimate criticism and slander is a very simple one and should be obvious. If I say that Grand Panjandrum X is a drunk, a swindler, or a half-Jew, or a government agent and *it isn't true,* then I am doing immense damage to the Movement and I am light-years out of line. If it is true, on the other hand, then it is Grand Panjandrum X who is out of order and shouldn't be anywhere near the Movement. I follow the Covington Method. If I *suspect* something, I investigate and I keep my mouth shut while doing so. If I find that my suspicions about a so-called "leader" are true, then I shout that truth from the rooftops, because the presence of creeps in the Movement is a matter of general concern and in many cases physical safety. I commend the Covington Method to you all.

It is difficult to assess precisely how much we have accomplished in the last thirty-odd years. It is true that we have wasted a lot of time, effort, and resources on various boondoggles and dead ends, but on the other hand there are some very clear indications beginning to emerge that it hasn't been a total waste. The split between racial nationalism and conservatism is now clear-cut and permanent. The Jewish question is now clearly to the forefront in the ideology and propaganda of virtually every group and publication. We have managed to shed a lot of cumbersome excess ideological baggage. There is a barely perceptible but definite increase in racial awareness among the young, and above all there is an almost overwhelming distrust of established authority prevalent all over White America. If the United States government were to tell White Americans that the sun was shining outside, very few would leave their homes without an umbrella.

One of the most hopeful developments is this automatic, assumed distrust and disbelief. The American people have been lied to so often by our political snake-oil salesmen that they no longer believe much of anything they are told, unless of course the Jews decide on a really major media offensive to sway White opinion. Even these are no longer totally effective, as witness the decay of interest and belief in the alleged "Holocaust". This means that they no longer believe everything they are told *about us,* among other topics. A chink in the enemy's armor, my brothers. Aim for it, widen it, exploit it! Remember, our people are slowly but surely developing an immunity to Judaeo-liberal crap. It takes a lot more of it, a much heavier dose, to produce the same degree of mental anesthesia among White working people than it took ten years ago. Given the financial competition now coming from the Arabs for media power and other means of communication and manipulation, the monetary outlay that the Jews have to invest in their propaganda machine increases every year and may yet become insupportable even for their vast bankrolls. This means a further slippage in their credibility and a further wearing-off of the crapulous mental anesthetic among our people.

How much of the growing racial ferment in America is the result of our own efforts and how much is the inevitable consequence of events is debatable. However, our contribution certainly hasn't hurt.

And what of the great White herd itself, the 150 million or so people from whom and for whom we must gain our victory? What kind of political condition are they in? Are they seething with discontent and ravening for revolution, just waiting for the signal to rise up and smash their oppressors?

No, and let us not kid ourselves that they are anywhere near that level of awareness. But if we work this thing right, *we can get there.*

It is up to us. From now on there must be no more excuses, no more lazy and dishonest casting of the blame upon the people themselves. White Americans agree, with ninety per cent of our philosophy and would support our programme *when those ideas are presented to them correctly* and when they are allowed to express their true viewpoint free from the threat of government or negroidal retaliation.

We assert that Whites are superior in intelligence, creativity, and moral character to the lesser races. What person genuinely objects to being told that he is a superior being? We claim that Whites in today's society are being treated with disgraceful injustice and unfairness because of a forcibly imposed "equality" which has no basis in nature or in the real world. White men can see this every day with their own eyes. We claim that negroids are detrimental to the quality of life and pose a physical threat to our people, especially our women and children who are smaller and weaker and therefore vulnerable to the more powerful congoid beasts. Again, our people are not blind. They see this for themselves and regulate their behavior accordingly, even if they are effectively forbidden to protest through fear of retaliation.

Comprehension: The function of the racial nationalist movement's propaganda is to express what our people feel in their hearts but which they cannot or will not articulate on their own.

Finally, there may in fact be a small glimmer of hope on the demographic front. For reasons best known to itself, the régime fails to publish complete and up to date statistics on racial breakdown and birth rate. However, there do seem to be some indications that while the Hispanic population growth is still going through the roof, the White birth rate is showing a slight turnaround and the negroidal birth rate is actually dropping due to increased abortions among nannies and the high death rate through homicide of young black males.

Better yet, what little evidence is available seems to imply that it is the better class of Whites who are reproducing, the workers and producers who are more racially aware. Liberals and Yuppies are having few babies, and when they do, their couples generally stop at one or two. Faggots and feminists, for obvious reasons, have no babies at all. The upper crud in general don't seem to be able to find time to fit child-bearing into their busy schedules of intrigue and dissipation. Sweeping generalizations along this line are risky and uncertain, but by and large the Whites who seem to be having children are the religious conservatives such as the Mormons and Biblical fundamentalists, the Identity Christians, and the largely Catholic blue-collar ethnics of the urban North and Midwest.

The present situation is unquestionably fraught with danger. But there is potential, there is hope, and there is a chance we can beat the scoundrels. *It is up to us.*

II.
WHY THE WHITE RESISTANCE HAS FAILED

Between December of 1980 and March of 1982 the government of the United States made four specific attempts to murder me, and after a while it started to get unnerving. I had applied for the renewal of my passport in the usual way and one day in September, 1981 it was hand-delivered by two 'droids in three-piece suits, one from the FBI and the other from the BATF, a rare example of fraternal cooperation between Uncle's lickspittle lackeys. These gentry laid the word on me in no uncertain terms. I was to depart the Land of The Free and the Home of the Brave, and that right speedily, or else they would have me arrested on some trumped-up charge and I would not survive my first night in the Federal holding facility. They were busy trying to frame the Greensboro men again on absurd "civil rights" charges and they had no intention of allowing me to become involved in any campaign against their grotesque show trials, much less testify on the stand as to my knowledge of the defendants' innocence and the BATF's guilt.

I stalled them for some months but after a final warning I decided to live to fight another day, and so I left. Now, I am bound and determined that this book is not going to become an autobiographical reminiscence of my wild and woolly past, so I won't get any further into the personal angle. But I was fortunate enough to end up in Ireland, and I brought away with me from the Emerald Isle one priceless asset that I can only thank Uncle and his 'droids for giving me. That asset is a first-class, first-hand political education on the realities of revolution. For the first time I *lived* in a White country which had gone through revolution within living memory and I saw at first hand the shape and texture of the thing, the errors and the potential errors committed both in 1920 and today in Northern Ireland, the reality of day-to-day life in a society wherein a revolutionary organization, leftist though it is, exerts pervasive and definite influence. In Rhodesia I learned the military arts of insurgency and counter-insurgency, but in Ireland I assimilated the political aspect.

I mention this so that my readers will have some idea with what authority I claim to speak on the subject. I will not cite my Movement experience because I am unable to appraise objectively my own political career. No man can judge himself fairly or present himself to others on the basis of his own self-estimation. I simply tell you that I have seen the finished product of a process which, allowing for the differences of culture and era, was approximately similar to what we are going to have to go through in this country. Ireland is not America, very true, but I've seen the elephant and I have a pretty good idea of what one is supposed to look like, so when I come to draw it from memory I have a distinct advantage over someone who has never seen an elephant at all.

On now to the topic at hand. The present day White resistance movement in America has its roots in the ashes of Berlin, and I do not except the Ku Klux Klan. The burning timbers of the Spree river bridges were still smoking and littered with the bodies of the teenaged *Hitler-jugend* defenders when American racial nationalists began organizing again. Gerald L. K. Smith, Conde McGinley, James Madole, Eustace Mullins, the Free Ezra Pound Committee, *Common Sense,* and hundreds of unknown activists left over from the Bund, the Coughlin movement, the America First Committee, the 1920s Klan, they all resumed the battle against a triumphant world Jewry and odds overwhelmingly hopeless. Later came the Minute Men; the various new Klan groups with tens of thousands of robed members; the Birch Society which, although co-opted by the enemy, served as a training ground for many of our best people; the Citizens' Councils; the Wallace movement; and over all the towering figure of Navy Commander George Lincoln Rockwell.

The cumulative effort that all these people and organizations have had on American White consciousness is problematical and debatable. I think the effect is there, we are beginning to see it, and will see more of it as the years progress. But in the main, the racial Right has *failed.* The Zionists are still in control. Whites are still losing ground everywhere, losing their jobs to affirmative action, losing their lives to non-white violence, losing their country to unassimilable aliens, losing their language to the yammer of the mud races. *Why have we failed?* Glad you asked, because I'm going to *tell* you why we have failed.

1. Disunity of purpose. It is too much to expect that in a country as huge and diverse as America, and in a population as variegated and individualistic as White Americans, there would be unity of organization, that is to say One Big Party. In actual fact it is probably just as well that there hasn't been such a party, because it would have been infiltrated and undermined from within as the Wallace movement was when it became a threat. But the various White groups have never been able to work together even tactically, for short periods of time, towards the most minor of local goals. Every attempt to bring about even temporary tactical unity has been a short-lived flop. Why?

Part of the reason is that White racial nationalists are the last of the true rugged individualists. The enemy periodically accuses us of being cranks and eccentrics and there is a certain element of truth to this. Our people are this society's genuine non-conformists, the real dissenters. This is because it is unpopular and actually unsafe to be a White racialist. There is no real dissent without danger. In today's America anybody can be a hippie, a Communist, a drug user (although pushers are officially considered "un-cool"), a sexual pervert, a voodoo cultist, a wigged-out Jesus freak, whatever. These things are socially acceptable. There is no real dissent in these activities, because the System encourages them as part of their efforts to demoralize and break down the White working class. There is no persecution of these people. Their life-styles are legal, even advocated, and regularly featured on the cover of *Newsweek.*

But dare to be a White racist, and brother you have got problems. You will lose your job, and there is not one goddamned law in all that mass of "civil rights" legislation that will protect your right to earn a living, or prevent you from being blacklisted in many areas. "Civil rights" are for people with hooked noses and faeces-colored skin, as you learn pronto. Your tires will be slashed and your car vandalized, and if you are politically active in your area the media will carefully print your address and splash your home all over page one and the television screen, deliberately targeting you for victimization, often nakedly and openly inciting it. Your insurance will be cancelled and you cannot replace your losses from enemy malice. You may well be evicted if you rent, when your landlord receives arson and bomb threats and decides that his property is more precious than your rights. Federal agencies will surveill you, follow you, tap your phone, open your mail, and possibly pay a professional liar to get up on a witness stand to swear your life away. Your friends and relatives all of a sudden won't touch you with a barge pole. Your wife eventually will crack under the strain and leave you, taking your children. You may well be murdered — the people who have come after me over the years have all been cowards and incompetents, but none of us can count on that kind of luck forever.

The White racial nationalist suffers for his beliefs and may well undergo martyrdom for them. It follows that it takes a very special kind of man or woman to willingly face these horrors, and the inner strength and toughness that sustains the individual activist does not always lend itself to teamwork and discipline. Hence much of the squabbling among the brethren. Proud, free Aryan spirits are hard to tame and break to harness, and if you know anything of our race's history you know this has always been so.

2. The Complete Lack of Any Serious Program. The first thing that strikes one when surveying the White resistance over the past decades is the invariable sense of *drift* that pervades the entire movement. Nobody seems to have a clear idea of just what they *want,* never mind how they are going to achieve it. There is a general agreement that we want certain things, true. We want our wives and our children to be able to walk the streets of America without getting butchered by wild animals. We want Big Brother off our backs. We want to he able to *keep* most of what we earn through our daily toil. We want our kids to be able to walk to a clean, safe, educationally sound neighborhood school that will teach them to read and write and not how to inject heroin into their veins or perform perversions on lovers of the same sex. We want to be able to live our lives from day to day without being confronted by gibbering black faces everywhere we turn. We want to keep faith with our friends overseas and actively resist Communism. We want a solid, loving family life with the husband and father as the head of the family and the wife and mother as its heart.

But as to *how* we will achieve all this? Most racial right programs and policies are confused, rhetorical, verbose, far too generalized, and sometimes go off on weird tangents regarding health foods and communication with beings from outer space. There is a conspicuous dearth of detail as to just *how* all these noble, uplifting, and praiseworthy programs are to be accomplished. (And to give them due credit, most of them *are* worthy and noble ideals if they could be attained.) This significant gap in the tapestry is something that virtually everyone who first comes into contact with the Movement notices very early on.

Party X has a program, an all-White America, a free enterprise economy, a sound money system, law and order, a halt to illegal immigration, dumping Israel — all the usual racial right standards. Let's say the program is a knockout, a real winner, just what the doctor ordered for America, and we need it implemented yesterday. A new member comes in and asks, "Great, what's the first step?" If he gets any reaction at all, it's one of three things:

* "Fill in this membership application, give us all the money in your wallet and a similar sum every month, go home, trust us, and wait for *The Day.*"

* "Put on this strange uniform or robe, displaying symbols and terminology that the American people have been conditioned from their cradles to reject. Go out into a public place with maybe a dozen other guys similarly attired, stand there waving a sign, and allow a mob of five thousand screaming Jews and Communists to pelt you with rocks, bottles, and garbage. During the course of this activity, your semi-retarded mini-führer will give a television interview which will then be edited by the station's news department to make him look like even more of an idiot than he probably is while simultaneously eliminating any good points he might make. Some of you may be arrested and have to spend every cent you make on lawyers for the next year while you pop in and out of the System's courtrooms on Mickey Mouse charges. Wow, what a victory for the race! Of course the American people just admire the hell out of this kind of bizarre behavior. We just *know* that one day they will rise up and join us in their millions. By the way, the slightest criticism of this insane tactic will lead to your instant expulsion from the party and brand you forever as yellow-bellied coward afraid to battle the enemy in the streets! Now, repeat five hundred times a day: It is 1932, It is 1932. It is 1932,' "(Or 'It is 1865' for Klan groups,)

* "First step? Duh——I dunno. You mean we are supposed to do somethin'? Well, hell, we did somethin' just last week! Had a meetin' and bad-mouthed niggers and Jews fer musta been three, four hours! Then we went down to the Dew Drop Inn and got drunk! How's that fer heavy duty political action, eh?"

To be fair, the great bulk of the White population does indeed respond to these tactics. They stay away from the racial right in droves.

Not everyone is an activist, to be sure. But some people *are* activists. They join the racial right because they want to work and fight for the race, and like all soldiers and would-be soldiers they get tired of waiting for orders that never come and give it up. I have never understood certain groups led by men I knew personally to be quite sincere and basically honest, if not necessarily brilliant, but who fail inaccountably to see the connection between belief and action. To me, it is quite obvious that if one *believes* in something one *acts* upon those beliefs. Is this such a difficult concept to grasp? Evidently so. *I* understand it, hopefully *you* understand it, and I know damned well the *enemy* understands it. And yet an awful lot of our erstwhile comrades seem to have missed the boat. They believe that to verbalize something is to solve it. The enemy cannot be talked down, he must be *put* down.

3. Many White "patriotic" groups are obvious frauds.

New members quickly tumble to the fact and leave.

I'm a bit at a loss to figure out just how to proceed on this subject. On the one hand, it is possibly the worst short and medium-range obstacle that the Movement faces; the vital funds and manpower which could make the difference in these crucial early stages are being blown away on paper fronts for thieves, and possibly worse than thieves. On the other hand, for the practical reasons I have cited before and also because this book is meant to be a positive instructional work and not a diatribe against any individual or group, I am going to have to resist the strong temptation to go off onto tirades every thirty pages about the pickpockets among us.

Yet it cannot be denied that one major reason for almost half a century of failure on our part has been the prevalence of fraudulent White organizations. There is also a very strong suspicion in the cases of several specific groups that the "leaders' were, or are, in the actual pay of the enemy and have been kept alive on financial life-support systems from the government and the ADL when contributions ran short. I can think of one former Klan leader and one proto-NS type who are proven agents and *have admitted the fact in open court,* in sworn statements, and have been exposed in the media. And yet I dare not name them here, not for any fear of the libel laws, but because *these men still have followers* who blindly refuse to accept any proof at all that their idol is a traitor. These followers buy books and my long-suffering publisher may not want to risk alienating his customers by "spreading disunity," i.e., letting me be so rude as to name in his publication men who have already been exposed.

Why, why, oh *why* are we so reluctant to deal with the phenomenon of the White right's frauds and swindlers? What, what, oh *what* does it take to finally discredit a "patriotic" phony? You'd think Billy James Hargis would have blown his gaff with his importation of gook orphans for White families to adopt and his "David and Jonathan" episodes with bum boys at his so-called "seminary." The jackass *still* has followers among the Christian racial right., (I'll try naming a few names and see if they appear in print.) You would think Bill Wilkinson's FBI file being printed all over the country in every major newspaper would have discredited him for good. Not a bit of it — up to the moment Wilkinson left for his next assignment he *still* had loyal Klansmen swearing by him. You would think Robert Welch's erratic behavior and repeated exposure by ex-John Birchers would have withered his congregation on the vine, but not at all. Welch still had fans until the day he died and, last I heard, there was someone or other in Belmont still running the Birch scam. You would think Willis Carto inserting Jews into key positions in Liberty Lobby and *SPOTLIGHT* might give people pause. Dream on — *SPOTLIGHT* is still the most widely read paper on the racial right and the one primarily responsible for propagating the lie that I am an ATF agent. (The author of the offending articles generally is a Jew named Herzberg.)

I could go on and on and on about this subject. *(Don't worry, you will. - Editor)* But are we surprised that the White right has failed with "leadership" such as this, and others I would give my eyeteeth to name who are much closer to home than the preceding little rogue's gallery?

4. Shortage of funds. Possibly "dispersion of funds" would be a better term. Every year millions of dollars are raised by strong conservative, anti-communist, and racial nationalist groups in this country. But if we say that ten million dollars a year are raised, then we must look at where that money goes. I would say at a guess that there are about two hundred groups competing for that money, and that annual sum is distributed widely and very unevenly. It is also used very inefficiently, and sometimes corruptly. Some organizations are a complete waste of every penny poured into them because their leadership is either dishonest or incompetent. Huge sums are also expended each year on every imaginable boondoggle and white elephant type of project, often in purest good faith but with nil results in the end. Con men aside, the Movement suffers from a chronic lack of administrative and financial expertise which prevents maximum utilization of the funds various groups do collect.

5. Single-issue politics. Many of the groups which have achieved a limited tactical success have been mono-line fronts or action committees dedicated to one single cause or problem to the exclusion of all others. There are anti-abortion groups; anti-homosexual groups; antidrug groups; associations which concentrate on one aspect of foreign policy such as South Africa or Nicaragua; tax rebellion groups who ignore the racial issue and racially oriented groups who ignore the economy; anti-Jewish groups who welcome non-Whites as members, and racist sects who actually admit Jews. All of this causes confusion, overlap, and duplication of effort, not to mention wasting time and money.

The problem of White recovery cannot be addressed on a piecemeal basis. The enemy uses their much-vaunted "salami tactics" to cut away our rights and our racial inheritance slice by slice, but although we may be able to restore them on a slice by slice basis, this will only be possible if we maintain an overall view of the big picture. Every issue facing our race interconnects. Every problem is inextricably linked with some other aspect, which in turn is linked to others. What is needed is a *Weltanschauung,* a world view, not just total concentration on abortion or tax reform.

6. Negative image problems. I never cease to be amazed at the sincere outrage many White activists express over the way we are treated by the media. "But that's not *true!*", these comrades wail at each fresh libel and smear. "That's not *fair!* It's not even accurate! And that reporter lady seemed so *nice!*"

OF COURSE THE MEDIA TELLS LIES! Great Jumping Jehosophat, my brothers, what the hell do you think the media *exist* for? To convey bona fide news and information? Think so? Then put down this book immediately and go search under your pillow for the money which the tooth fairy left you last night.

Comprehension: The media are the primary weapons the System uses against White people. In any future struggle against a non-Constitutional regime, the media's plant and personnel are legitimate military targets.

One television camera is worth a hundred tanks, a division of niggerized Federal troops, a dozen atomic warheads. The worth of television and cinema, and, to a lesser extent the printed media, to our enemies is beyond calculation. Twenty million black and Puerto Rican and lesbian soldiers in OD green could not keep our people enslaved if the power of the silver screen were broken. And yet a minuscule number of television technicians and newscasters, assisted by a somewhat larger number of newspaper and magazine manipulators, have kept the White man anesthetized and powerless while he is being slowly destroyed.

And we wonder why we can't seem to get a fair shake in the media, when one of the media's prime tasks is to present negative images of White dissent and those who practice it?

7. Failure to Communicate. Our message is all too often couched in obscure language, religious dialectic and Scriptural passages which may or may not be relevant, overly complex terminology, or downright gibberish. We assume that our White listeners know all about things like the Jewish origin of Communism, or the Soviet wheat scam, or the Masonic conspiracy, or the Holocaust hoax. They don't. To be perfectly candid, them honkies don't know nuttin. Bear in mind that we are not talking to Europeans or to products of a European educational system which still produces literate and partially knowledgeable adults capable of comprehending reasoned argument even if incapable of assimilating it. We are talking to Ronald McDonald. *Boobus Americanus* doesn't know a *Weltanschauung* from a willie. He wants his politics packaged in styrofoam and guaranteed 100% content-free, just like his Big Mac.

And thus we are going to have to package our message. Many of us, including myself, don't like this idea one bit. But my brothers, I tried for nine long years to get through to my own people using the approach which I still feel to be morally correct, the open National Socialist approach with which I still feel most comfortable. And I had some success. But not enough. Like many of you, I will find Big Mac politics distasteful and repugnant, but then we're not in this to edify our own pristine sensibilities, are we? At least I'm not.

I did not mean to do our people an injustice when I said that they knew nothing. I was simply stating a fact. But while they may *know* nothing, they feel much. Knowledge can be concealed and distorted by false teaching. Truth can be withheld. But instinct can never be entirely suppressed even by the most rigorous psychological and cultural conditioning. White Americans still have basically sound instincts and it is this fact we must rely on as a basis for our efforts to communicate. Deep down, do any of our people really *like* niggers? Hell, *niggers* can't stand niggers. Oh, maybe there are a few druggies and psychopaths who honestly believe in their heart of hearts that these creatures are in some manner "equal." But while our people as a whole may be politically ignorant, they're not stupid. Way, deep down, maybe so far down they don't even know they know it, I think every man and woman of our race savvies what the score is. They are just waiting for someone to articulate it in the way they themselves cannot. We must constantly bear in mind, though, just how low we must shoot in order to make a hit.

III.
HOW THE WHITE RESISTANCE WILL WIN

The chapter heading here is neither overly optimistic nor is it mere revolutionary hyperbole. I am personally convinced that we will indeed win in the end. We will win because in the final analysis we are smarter, morally and mentally tougher, meaner, and just plain better than our enemies. Bear in mind that the White race has only been losing ground since the early part of this century and that for three thousand years prior to that we walked through the valley of the shadow of death fearing no evil because we were the meanest SOBs in the valley. Victory is in our genes and given half a chance those Viking and Conquistador chromosomes will re-assert themselves.

The big question is how much political, economic, social, and genetic damage we are going to suffer before we *do* get our act together. The price we have paid for three generations of Judeo-Liberalism and material luxury is tragically steep enough already, yet we may have to pay a more fearsome price still, and if we pay, the whole world pays with us. Remember that the future of this planet and the entire humanoid species depends on the re-assertion of White order and authority over the globe. How will this come about, you ask? Just how are we going to raise ourselves out of the muck and slime into which the Jews and our own laziness and hedonism have cast us? Glad you asked. I will now proceed to *tell* you how we are going to win.

The first thing we are going to do is to *refuse to give up.* We will never, ever accept the racial enemy's victory as anything more than a temporary aberration of history, a geopolitical burp in the fabric of mankind's development. Never, *ever* will we accept racial integration, miscegenation, left-wing social experimentation, degeneracy, and neo-Marxism as "inevitable," You will notice that the main thrust of enemy propaganda is always just that, the alleged "inevitable" and inexorable nature of their so-called "progressive" change. Always there is the refrain, the complaint of why can't us honkies realize it's all pre-ordained, written in the stars? Why can't we just relax and let our little honky minds just drift away as we slowly bleed to death in this luxurious hot bath of filth and glittering trash that the Jews have allowed us to wallow in? Why wave those Confederate flags, those horrible Swastikas, those antique flaming crosses? Isn't it pitiful in a way, Hymie? The *goyim* actually think they *can do* something about it all! What fools! Don't they know it's all inevitable?

HORSE HOCKEY! The destruction of the White race is *not,* repeat, not in any way inevitable, pre-ordained, or even likely! There are still enough of us left to reverse the process of genocide and turn the tables on our enemies. It's true we are outnumbered, but there's an Afrikaans proverb to the effect that one lion can slay a whole troop of baboons. The enemy have the numbers, true, but we have the quality if we can awaken enough of our brothers and bring that superiority to bear. A hundred years ago, small handfuls of White men armed with iron will, inflexible purpose, and the fruits of White creativity and craftsmanship laid all of Africa and most of Asia at the feet of Aryan man. It can and will be done again. Because we *will not give up!*

The racial enemy has three things on his side. First off, he has vastly superior numbers with which he may well attempt to overrun the White world in a "Camp of the Saints" type scenario. So far he has held off from orchestrating such a massive migration because he realizes that Whites are still necessary to maintain production and order. The Japanese and Koreans and other Asiatics are presently being groomed to take over this type of vitally necessary function, and once the Jew feels sufficiently certain that his fellow Orientals can make the cars and computers, run them, and keep the wogs in line, then the physical invasion of the White world will probably be escalated. Actual physical admixture between the White race and assorted blacks and browns is a vital linchpin of the genocide program; the more the better from the Jew's point of view, so long as goods and services are maintained and a minimum of order necessary to protect the Jews themselves is kept up.

The second thing the enemy has on his side is money, i.e., the goods and services which money can buy. This includes the physical plant of White repression — the computers and police equipment and television cameras and prisons and so on — plus the skilled mercenary personnel and tame non-Whites to man and operate the apparati of control. In this society, money is equivalent to political power, in that it enables its possessor to bring about actual change. Bear in mind that much of the enemy's tactics, such as legal harassment, will be designed to deplete our own tiny reserves of this precious, vital resource. Many fraudulent White "patriotic" groups have been set up and no doubt still operate for the dual purpose of discrediting the cause through bad propaganda and through siphoning away donations from legitimate groups.

The third leg of the deadly tripod upon which the enemy's power rests is *mind control,* meaning all the various media and the thousand and one ways the media anesthetize, manipulate, and direct the minds of White people. So long as the masses of White people will obey the régime because they have been brainwashed by the goggle box, we will get nowhere. We all know and fear the power of the monstrous tube and its ancillary movie, video, rock music, sports, and printed tentacles. The lives of White revolutionaries in these times are like a Grade D video nasty where a small band of normal people flee through an eternal night surrounded by the Living Dead who have risen from their graves and stumble around everywhere clawing at us and making grunting noises.

The enemy has many more deadly items in his bag of tricks, to be sure, but knock those three legs of the unholy tripod out from under him and he's going down with a resounding crash. How do we do this? How do we counteract these three overwhelmingly powerful weapons trained against us?

First off, as regards the enemy's oceanic reserve of limitless non-White numbers, bear in mind that from his point of view this is not an unmixed blessing. Although a steady stream of non-Whites is being fed into the White world where they can and do contaminate the Aryan gene pool as it is intended they should, the vast bulk of all the world's non-Whites are still in their own areas of the globe and exist in a very primitive and unrefined state. It would be very difficult even for an apparatus as powerful as that which the world's ZOGs have established to actually bring these numbers to bear where they would do the most damage to the White gene pool. For instance, how would the Washington ZOG justify bringing in ten million Hindus to Wyoming and Montana or Iowa where too many White babies are being born for their liking? White America has of course been subjected to a slow intravenous drip of non-Whites for many years, but like arsenic or antimony, the poison has built up to a painful and dangerous level and the "patient" is beginning to feel the sickness and the irritation even through his heavy boob-tube anesthetic. So remember, it's not how many non-Whites there *are* in the world, but how many the enemy can directly *bring to bear* on any given White group or nation. The figures are still disquieting, true, but not quite as overwhelming as a first glance at world demographics might suggest.

Also bear in mind that the massive world reserve of non-Whites is costing the ZOGs of North America and Europe a pretty penny to maintain. Right now all they do is eat, breed, and slaughter one another in large numbers while draining Yehudi's wallet of funds that might otherwise be turned directly against us. In addition, many Third World dictatorships are starting to get ideas above their station and bite the hand that feeds them, the hand being that of ZOG, even if the bread comes from White America's labor and productivity. Non-Whites are notoriously difficult to discipline, especially the black and brown ones, and the Anglo-Zionist international enforcement apparati such as the IMF, Bilderbergers, etc., are starting to get hostile vibes off them jungle drums in the Third World boondocks. ZOG has already had to spend a lot of time and effort putting out bush fires in places like the Philippines, Nicaragua, Angola, Ethiopia, South Korea, etc. The Japanese especially are exhibiting a very disturbing tendency to think independently and an appalling readiness to actually criticize the Jews. This stroppiness from the Asiatic nation being groomed to replace White America's productivity and infrastructure must be very unnerving indeed in high Zionist circles. Yehudi may well find his mud-colored "population bomb" blowing up in his own face before he can lob it at us.

The second leg of that infernal tripod is *money.* This is going to be possibly the worst one to battle and defeat, because it is the area in which we are most vulnerable ourselves. They can't force us to mate with mud people, they can't brainwash or re-condition the minds of revolutionaries once those minds have been freed, but they can damned sure defunctionalize us and make sure that we are ineffective through lack of funds.

The whole topic of Movement finance is one which must be dealt with separately. We will talk about our money later; right now let's discuss *their* money, There are many racial right people who have devoted their entire political careers to analysing and documenting the enemy's money, what he does with it and how he does it. If you are one of the people for whom this book is intended, you will probably be familiar with the economic aspects of the world problem; if not, then I just don't have time to give you a long dissertation on the whys and wherefores of money, its use and abuse. Go to the source from which you obtained *The March Up Country* and chances are you will be able to get more reading matter on the subject.

Basically, *money itself is not an inherently evil concept.* It was historically inevitable when barter became too complicated and the range of available goods and services grew with man's development. However, some thousands of years before Christ, our little friends the Jews invented a neat scam to make money reproduce itself. This scam, which is at the root of all economic evil to this very day, is called *interest.* The money which is accrued through interest isn't really money, it is a phantasm. True money has meaning only insofar as it represents an existing item of wealth or a service which cannot be conveniently carried in the pocket or the pouch — a goat, ten arrowheads, an acre of land, a set of tools to make real things with, a service such as the tilling of land or the filling of a tooth. Money that represents only more money is an absurdity, and yet it is upon this absurdity that our economy is built. I do not except gold and silver, because these are simply metals that society has been persuaded to value in themselves, and rather soft, useless metals at that. One cannot eat a gold piece, one can't roof one's house in gold, one cannot chop firewood with silver or shoot it at one's enemies (unless you're hunting werewolves.)

The preceding is the theory, but in practice money makes the world go 'round and as far as we are concerned this is likely to be the operative situation in our lifetimes. What we all need to understand, though, is that the Federal Reserve notes we are paid with and with which we in turn pay the rent and purchase our six-pack are not real money in the sense that they represent any concrete value in themselves. They are simply pieces of rather drably-printed paper. They are worth only what the other people we must deal with *think* they are worth. What determines this generally accepted level of value? Why does your landlord consider your apartment to be worth $350 a month? Why not $50, or $5, or $5000? Why does the convenience store charge you $3.99 for that six-pack? Why not 39 cents or $39? Everyone determines the price he charges for his goods, services, and labor on the basis of what *he himself must pay* for the goods and services he needs. If A charges B $50 for a real item or a service, B charges C $50 for an equivalent item or service, C charges D $50 and so on. If A ups his price to $55, or $60, or $75, then everyone passes along that cost until you have to fork over more yourself for your apartment rent and your six-pack. Whereupon *you* then charge Mr. A more for whatever goods or services you provide *him,* and the whole process begins again. This, my brothers, is known as an *inflationary spiral,* and it is the way we will smash the money power of the Jews.

How does such a spiral get started? Simple. Someone along the long, infinitely complex chain is bad at managing his money or else has unexpected expenses, and so he attempts to recoup his losses from the next man in the economic circuit, and thus the process begins. Now, one landlord or convenience store upping prices won't start an economic tailspin. Where do major economic upheavals begin? They are rooted in two causal factors: *worldwide economic trends* and *governmental incompetence.* Sometimes the inflationary spiral can be started by a cut in a critical commodity such as oil or grain or iron ore, the failure of a crop or a Third World war that interdicts a vital resource. But mostly inflation is caused by governments through economic and financial mismanagement, which almost always means deficit spending, either outright deficit or through borrowing.

Right now the United States is carrying the biggest deficit in the history of human civilization on this planet. The numbers are in the trillions of dollars, but at this point they really mean nothing. What it all amounts to is that the régime here, in order to support the burden of non-White welfare, plundering by the ruling élite, and economic incompetence and malfeasance on a scale beyond imagining, has simply given up all pretense of balancing the budget, living within our means, and basing our money on any kind of actual production or real wealth. The U.S. government is simply spending whatever it feels like spending on anything and the Jews of the Federal Reserve are just rolling those presses and cranking out them greenback dollars. So far the incredible wealth and diversity of the North American continent, combined with the superb productivity and skill of the White American worker, has kept the bubble from bursting. My guess is that the great White blue-collar Atlas can still carry this world on his shoulders for some time longer, but eventually something's got to give.

The maintenance of the present System calls for money, money, ever more money, an endless flow of green dollars to keep the creaking machinery greased, buy toys for the Yuppies and drugs for the non-Whites, keep them welfare checks rolling off the computer printers and keep the mercenary SWAT teams on call to quell disturbances. There are massive foreign aid programs which must be bankrolled, vital towards keeping the wogs in line. There are massive subsidies to be paid to inefficient unionized industries, to keep the Northern White blue-collar workers in line. There are ATF and FBI offices to be staffed and mercenaries in three-piece suits to be paid, informers to be bribed, and prisons to be maintained in order to keep the Southern Whites in line. There are massive media propaganda campaigns to be financed in order to keep fifty different special interest groups in line and advance the causes of another fifty special interest groups. Rich as America is, we long ago stopped producing enough wealth to pay for this extravagant and corrupt System. So the printing presses at the Federal Reserve roll on.

The resources of the System are already strained near the breaking point. One of our primary strategic goals, my brothers, must be to put ever more strain on the enemy's pocketbook. His bureaucratic arteries are clogged, his muscles attenuated and decrepit if still powerful, and his whole machinery of administration is vitally dependent on the green-ink fuel of money in order to function. Make him spend, brothers, make him spend! He can take from us our tens of thousands of dollars by dragging us in and out of his courtrooms, by getting us fired from our jobs and defunctionalized, by harassing us with tax bills and other tactics. But we can make him spend millions and millions if we plan carefully, move fast, hit hard, and *THINK!*

The Greensboro shootings cost us tens of thousands, true, and placed sixteen fine men at deadly risk. But how much did it cost the enemy, other than five dead pets? It cost them millions in court costs, police and Federal agency overtime, bribes to informers, more bribes in unsuccessful attempts to suborn perjury, the media coverage, the security for subsequent Red demonstrations and negroidal carry-on, the "civil rights commission" hearings, etc. In the late 1970s, how much did Operation Skokie cost the enemy in money terms? How much financial damage did the Order do in the early 1980s? How much money does the enemy invest every year in on-going investigation, harassment, and containment of the racial right?

How much money would it cost this System to fight off any kind of widespread, outright White insurrection? How much for police overtime and danger pay, for troops, supplies, logistics, intelligence, prisoner maintenance? How much money would the enemy lose due to strikes by the productive White working people? How much would security for politicians and bureaucrats to protect them from assassination cost? How much would the massive concomitant media propaganda campaign cost? How much more would they have to pay their White mercenaries once suppressing White revolutionaries became physically dangerous? How much money would they lose through uncollected taxes and destroyed tax records? How much would they lose through Federal resignations for health reasons and inability to replace the lost personnel at any cost? How much in widows' pensions and benefits would they have to pay out? How much in VA benefits to their own surviving casualties? How much money would they have to divert from other projects with subsequent economic and political loss? How much would they lose to various kinds of discontent from the non-White minorities who would necessarily catch the brunt of the insurrection from both sides?

The previous scenario is, of course, purely hypothetical. But bear in mind, my brothers, that while we cannot afford to lose the hundreds and thousands of dollars that they exact from us, the millions we can and do cost them ain't chicken feed either. And what will be their solution? Let them printing presses roll, crank out them green pieces of paper! The result? An inflationary spiral that will cripple the enemy more than any bomb or gun or strike we could come up with.

The third leg of the unholy tripod is the tube, and to a lesser extent the printed media, the music industry, and so on. Breaking the power of the silver screen is going to be hard, to be sure, and for a long time we will not be able to discern much progress. But it can be done, I assure you.

In a military situation against an unconstitutional tyranny, as opposed to the quasi-constitutional one we have now, dealing with the tube will be simplified because we will be able to deal directly with the personnel who man the cameras and provide the faces and voices. At a later stage, the military arm of the resistance should also be able to compel a sense of balance and accuracy in the cinematic and other media apparati. I suspect that a short glance down the wrong end of a .44, an experience rather like staring down the mouth of the Holland Tunnel, will be enough to make the most left-wing of Hollywood producers see the light, thus damming the flow of anti-White flicks from MGM and Universal. Deprived of their main propaganda weapons in the media, or at least deprived of their 100% effective use through military action, the System will be limping from the beginning when the shooting finally starts.

The problem is going to lie in the initial political phases of the revolutionary struggle, when we are still constrained by the "legality" which compels us to play by the rules which the System ignores at will. This is when the power of the media will be brought to bear against us with potentially overwhelming force. We must plan very carefully how we are going to deal with this protracted deluge of faecal matter which is going to be dumped all over us from the goggle box, the video, the radio, and the movie screen. Make no mistake, despite the White public's growing skepticism about anything they are told from "official" sources, they are still very susceptible indeed to the many subtle and subliminal techniques the media use to manipulate their minds and control their thoughts.

The first thing that the White revolutionary movement must do is to *build our own lines of communication,* not only with one another between our diverse groups and cells, but build channels of communication *from the Movement directly to the White population* . The main thrust of our political work must always be to circumvent the enemy media and get our racial and political message *directly to the White community* without filtering it through the electronic and printed apparati where what we say is edited, distorted, selectively presented, or censored.

In the beginning of our organizing activities we must avoid the media like the plague, just as we avoid entanglements with the enemy's police and courts. This serves the dual purpose of protecting our activists from identification and subsequent victimization, and also protecting the White community in the area from enemy disinformation about our program and our aims.

Later on it can become politically expedient to attempt to use the media for propaganda purposes in order to advance our cause. However, this is a very technical and complex subject on its own, a revolutionary skill that requires finesse, tact, dissimulation, and a very fine sense of timing and effect. It is not to be undertaken lightly, nor is it to be undertaken at all except in very special circumstances. Any attempt at using the media can always backfire. Remember: the enemy are not fools, and media people will probably be more clever than most, especially the White renegades who comprise a high percentage of their forward personnel.

The Tools of Victory

The obvious requirement necessary to bring about change is state power. That is to say, White racial nationalist revolutionaries must organize to seize the institutions and instruments of government and use those same institutions and apparati to undo what the enemy has done. One would think that this concept is so basic, so self-evident, that it need not even be articulated.

Wrong. Most racial right programs don't even mention state power. How on earth could something like that happen? How is it possible for

White racial nationalist groups to function year in and year out, issuing newspapers and newsletters, holding meetings, formulating programs, raising funds, passing out leaflets, staging public rallies, and never *mentioning the one essential for victory?* Never mentioning political state power at all? Never even hinting at how they hope to bring about the change they claim to advocate? Don't ask me, people. It has always flabbergasted me. The only thing I can suggest is that fraud is very common indeed on the White right, as I have said before. I'm not going to spend any more time arguing this particular point. Anyone who believes that any major lasting change can be achieved while the enemy still controls the apparatus of state is so far out of it he's useless in any case.

The first tool necessary to seize state power is *a White revolutionary party,* a body I will henceforth refer to as a WRP. It need not be called a "party" as such. It may be a "Front," a "Union," a "Congress," even, God help us, a "club." Call it what you will, you must have a body of men and women working towards the same goal and under some tenuous discipline. The WRP may evolve into a tightly disciplined and monolithic party like Lenin's Bolsheviks. It may be a coalition of disparate groups with different outlooks and emphases. It may be a formless mass distinguished only by a vague name. It may embody all of these foregoing aspects, changing chameleon-like as circumstances dictate.

I am not going to sit here and pontificate about the White revolutionary party in America and what shape it may take in the future. I imagine it will run the gamut of every conceivable structure, strategy, and format. But I will tell you what the bona fide White revolutionary party *will not, can not* be like. These negatives are vital, because they have to do with the WRP's chances of victory.

The White revolutionary party must first of all be *White,* that is to say that its membership must be comprised entirely of White people, its program must be aimed solely towards the benefit of the White race, and non-Whites must be completely excluded from every aspect of organization and ideology. You would think, again, that this would be obvious. Apparently not. I have known otherwise sincere White racial nationalists who passionately advocate alliances with non-Whites, a tragic execrable admission of utter weakness. I have seen niggers wearing Third Reich Nazi uniforms and attending allegedly NS meetings *(I kid you not!).* I have seen "good Jews," i.e., allegedly repentant Jews, wanting to make up for their people's crimes, addressing allegedly racial nationalist meetings. I have seen the organizers of White "patriotic" functions send coffee and doughnuts out to nigger cops watching the proceedings, just waiting for orders to come in and commit violence against the participants. I have seen so-called "White patriots" angling for nigger votes. I have known so-called White racists who were married to Orientals or had brown-skinned girl friends.

What can I say about all this? I don't know. Words fail me. *Need* I say anything about it? Does it really call for any comment? Am I the only one who can see anything wrong with inviting non-Whites into the ranks?

Let me attempt to explain something very basic. White people are *White* people, non-White people are *not. Got* that? Or would you like for me to repeat it? A person is White or non-White due to his ancestry, his genes, his chromosomes. *Race is biological.* That means it is hereditary. It is something you are born with, and that you cannot change. You can't stop being White and a nigger can't start. Neither can an Oriental. The contents of that nigger's brain, his thoughts, his utterances, are of no consequence whatsoever. He may genuinely believe in racial separation. More power to him if he does. Let him demonstrate his beliefs by staying separate, or better yet, voluntarily repatriating himself to Africa. He is a very switched-on spade but he is not our friend, not our ally, and not our comrade. He is not of our race. He has nothing to do with us. Let him be elsewhere.

If we White racial nationalists are so damnably weak, so powerless, so flaccid, that we must in some manner ally ourselves with any kind of racial mud whatsoever, then we need to hang it up, disband our various groups and organizations, and get on with the business of dying. We have failed if we cannot prevail on our own, alone, strictly seg. If we have to use non-White numbers, non-White racial solidarity, and non-White dislike of mankind's universal enemy the Jew, in order to advance our own ideas, then our ideas aren't worth advancing. Let's leave it to the Black Muslims and go get drunk. The mere fact that I should have to interrupt this book for a digression like that indicates just how badly wrong some things in this Movement are.

But before I leave this subject, I'm going to try a specific example, to illustrate just how this idiocy can sift into racial nationalist politics. If it gets bowdlerized then so be it; many of my readers will know that I am referring to the inimitable master of Movement flummery, the Romany Führer himself, In the late 1970s, the "Führer" got a hot flash on a scam to get hold of some of the big bucks available in Florida's Cuban community for anti-Communist causes. He got hooked up with a couple of passably White Cubans in Miami and formed something called the National Socialist Cuban Legion. This thingie never did much of anything, although a couple of Cubans did come up to the "Führer's" headquarters and get their pictures taken, wearing Swastika armbands, shaking hands with the Great Man. From what I gather, even some of the "Führer's" staunchest supporters found this blatant multi-racialism a bit much to swallow and whatever greenbacks the Cubans did stump up evidently didn't compensate for the numbers of NSWPP members who resigned in disgust.

But let us say that one day the "Führer's" man in Havana, Juan Mendez, comes up to headquarters from Miami bringing a visitor. Juan himself is visually White, understand. He introduces his companion to the Great Man, "Commandante, thees is my cousin Carlos Mendez. He have jus' escape from preeson in Cuba. He sail all the way to Key West on two oil drums. He spend fifteen year in Castro's preeson for shooting Communistas. He is brave anti-Communist fighter, so let us welcome heem into de party." Now, I've no doubt in the world cousin Carlos is a brave anti-Communist fighter. *Nobody* likes living under Communism, and spics are no exception. Just one slight problem — cousin Carlos is also black as the ace of spades. The Great Man turns green and flees to his inner sanctum upstairs, leaving a couple of puzzled Cubans sitting in the literature room.

The point I am attempting to make here is that some kinds of ideological compromise lead to a slippery slope that will eventually land White revolutionaries in the trash compactor. We have got to learn the difference between *tactical* compromise and minimal *ideological principle.* Knowing which is which is sometimes difficult, I agree. But certain things are beyond the pale, and fraternization with non-Whites is surely one of them. As to the old question of how one decides just who is White? Simple.

COMPREHENSION: For our purposes, determining who is White involves the benefit of the doubt. We give none. If there is any reasonable doubt at all about a man's or woman's racial antecedents, exclude them. The slightest doubt isn't worth any possible contribution a racially marginal individual might make.

The second necessary aspect of the WRP is that it is revolutionary, that is to say that it seeks a *completely new* social order. It does not seek to reform the present corrupt system. It does not seek to participate in the ritualistic mumbo-jumbo of System politics. It recognizes that the present régime is totally corrupt and totally tainted and completely beyond redemption. It understands that the United States Constitution has been so distorted by judicial and governmental abuse that it is now unworkable in its present form. Under no circumstances whatsoever does the White revolutionary compromise or exercise moderation. Moderation in pursuit of White Power is a betrayal of every White man and woman who has suffered and died at the hands of the enemy.

The White revolutionary party is *selective in its membership.* It ensures that those who work for its goals and those who represent its ideals to the White community reflect those ideals in their own lifestyle and their own presentation. The WRP does not tolerate within its ranks those who are unwilling or unable to discipline themselves and regulate their behavior in order to bring themselves into conformity with the principles of White Power and common decency.

The White revolutionary party is *exclusive.* It demands, and receives, the complete and total allegiance of its members and their loyalty to the exclusion of all other White organizations. A WRP is not a Chinese menu, where one picks something from column A and something from column B and dessert from column C. The party demands, and receives, every ounce of effort and support which the member has to offer the Movement. Dabblers, dilettantes, and hobbyists are barred from association with the WRP and are purged ruthlessly when they creep in despite all efforts. Conservatives are banned and derided with the same vigor as homosexuals, race-mixers, and other degenerates. The WRP has no wish to *conserve* anything. It wishes to level the present society to its very foundations and then rebuild upon the ruins.

The White revolutionary party is the primary tool we will use to bring about our victory and our new age leading to the Aryan Imperium which will be mankind's highest expression of its destiny. There will be more than one such party, in more than one country. Each WRP will have some different characteristics and a somewhat different development, but the successful ones will adhere to the rules I have just outlined. How the revolution itself will progress is the topic for the next chapter.

IV.
FOUR PHASES TO VICTORY

I would like to remind my readers once again that this book is not intended to be some kind of Holy Writ that is engraved in granite. It is merely intended to get our people to start using their noggins and to circulate some ideas for discussion within the Movement. I don't want to start laying down the law and asserting that the White revolution *will absolutely* be like such and such and *must* be like such and such. I might be wrong.

I am convinced that the White revolution, when it occurs, will happen partially due to a combination of favorable circumstances and partially because a WRP has planned and laid groundwork for years to prepare itself to take advantage of just such a set of circumstances. But I could be in error. There might be some massive calamity that sweeps away the System as effectively as any man-made insurrection. We might get outside aid that enables us to slice years off the timetable, although right now I haven't a clue where such aid might come from. Aliens from Alpha Centauri, perhaps, or I suppose in a pinch I could always sell my soul to Old Nick in exchange for a White revolution. (A bargain. I'd make in a heartbeat if I could be convinced that I would ensure the perpetual survival of the White race for all time by doing so.) Kidding aside, there are things which may yet occur which might radically alter the whole equation and render this entire book obsolete.

COMPREHENSION: Every revolution is a hybrid, a mutant. While there may be some similarities to other revolutions which have occurred previously in other ages and places, each time the ingredients are in different proportion, the spices and garnishes different, the cooking time and temperature making it a whole new recipe. We can be guided to some extent by those who have gone before, but not completely, not always. Never be afraid to improvise.

Every revolution also has a series of crucial turning points, places identifiable to the later historian who can then argue, "This is where they went wrong," or "This is where they got it right," Every revolution has a spark, a combustion like the turning of an ignition switch when all of a sudden it was alive, running, moving. Our revolution will succeed, if for no other reason than the moral certainty of God's intention that our race survive. When the historians of future centuries sit down to write of the revolutions which saved the White race, I am convinced that in each White nation, allowing for a wide degree of environmental and circumstantial variance, the story will always read more or less like this:

PHASE ONE: Initial Cadre Recruitment

The White revolutionary party (WRP) will begin with a small, hard core of ideologically motivated individuals who draw their inspiration from their country's nationalistic history and from the great awakenings of the late nineteenth and early twentieth centuries in Europe. While these people may initially be merely nationalist or proto-Fascist and authoritarian, they will all eventually acknowledge the primacy of National Socialism and the Führer Adolf Hitler, at least in the privacy of their own thoughts. They will march under many banners, many names, many programs, and adopt many disguises and camouflages, but in their hearts will ring the immortal Song of a young German street fighter named Horst Wessel. Bitterly, regretfully, reluctantly we must acknowledge the accomplished fact that the one true Banner cannot be hoisted at the moment. There is simply too much at stake for us to give that kind of an edge to the enemy right from the very start. The Leader himself would be the first to tell us this. That mightiest of all Aryan souls desires for our race to live in freedom and in glory, not to die wrapped in the faded trappings that the Reich's valiant warriors wore.

And so we will settle for lesser but still proud and glorious banners and symbols — my own crimson Stars and Bars, the green of Ireland, the lion standard of Scotland, the colors of the White man's newest nations such as Australia and South Africa, emblems and totems from our racial past and ones yet to be invented. Who knows? Maybe one day the Green and White may fly yet again over Cecil Square in Salisbury. I would like to believe so. But whatever names, whatever symbols, whatever flags we march and fight beneath, always there will be the little private gatherings and toasts on April the 20th and November the 9th. *Und Ihr habt doch gesiegt, Kameraden.*

This small group of people will get together and determine that something must be done. They will then begin to contact, feel out, and recruit other like-minded individuals. There will be virtually nothing in the way of formal organization at this stage, just a group of people who hold similar views who correspond, meet together, and discuss certain things. Every person initiated into this select circle will be of the highest intelligence, dedication, and personal integrity. Every person initiated into this circle will complete a basic course of reading, studying, and ideological development if they have not done so already. Every person within this small, select circle will be in basic agreement with a few fundamental principles and will be willing to actively work to put those principles into action.

A certain rudimentary organization will appear during the latter stages of Phase One. In each locality one or two people will sort themselves out as generally recognized, if not formalized cell or section leaders. Basic operational tactics within each locality where the circle is active will be decided upon. Certain rudimentary supplies and items of equipment such as paper, printing plant, and secret office and warehouse space will be identified, located, and lined up.

Towards the very last *a name* of some sort will be decided upon for use during the forthcoming operations of Phase Two. This name will be necessary purely to separate the WRP's people from the people of other White organizations and to exact the necessary degree of exclusivity from those people who enter the WRP's circle. The name may or may not be the name used in Phases Three and Four. Since it is purely for identification purposes, it may be something completely innocuous like the "All American Chowder Society" or the "Committee for Policy Studies" or whatever. The ultimate example of this is the designation adopted by the Mafia in the 1930s, *La Cosa Nostra,* which in Sicilian dialect means simply, "This thing of ours". There will be no membership lists, no membership cards, no uniform or badges, no official titles or job descriptions at this stage. The head man of the WRP, for such a person there must be, will have no grandiose designation such as Generalissimo or Grand Panjandrum; he will simply be "Joe" or "Fred".

The circle of activists will quietly, efficiently prepare themselves psychologically and materially for a life of struggle and conflict. They will pay off as many of their debts as possible, clear their mortgages if they can, prepare contingency plans for when they are captured or when they must go on the run. They will clear the decks and tie down as many loose ends as they can so that the enemy will have as little to grab onto as possible. They will prepare alternative economic plans in order to sustain themselves in the likely event they are identified by the enemy too early on and defunctionalized, fired from their jobs and banned from further "legitimate" employment. They will educate themselves and prepare themselves psychologically and spiritually for life on the fringes of so-called "normal" society, the life of the outlaw and heretic. They will make their wills.

PHASE TWO:
Groundwork in the General Population

During Phase One the White revolutionary party will have prepared a program and a basic line of propaganda aids such as leaflets, marginal impedimenta such as stickers and envelope stuffers, tracts and pamphlets, basically things to catch the attention of potential supporters and activists and get them interested. Phase Two will begin with the WRP inaugurating an outreach program in order to recruit, educate, and motivate new activists *drawn directly from from White community,* people with little or no prior history of political involvement. Throughout Phase Two this type of selective, careful recruiting will take place. With very few exceptions indeed, no one will join the WRP on application — that's how informers and *agents provocateur* get in. The WRP *will invite new people to join,* after lengthy and careful indoctrination, examination, and scrutiny of the prospective member's lifestyle and character.

The purpose of Phase Two will be to prepare the WRP to *engage the enemy* during Phase Three, that is to say, begin open agitational propaganda and a political assault on the institutions and apparati of enemy power. It is arguably the most crucial of the four phases, because the WRP will stand or fall due to the strength or the weakness of its work during Phase Two.

How many people will need to be recruited as cadres during Phase One? During Phase Two? How long will Phase One last? How long before sufficient Phase Two preparation has been completed to "go public" and initiate open political struggle? Hell, I don't know. How long is a piece of string? In most cases the WRPs in question won't even be designating these phases in the same way I am designating them here. I am referring to the way a successful White revolutionary movement will develop organically. I will add, though, that my guess is different sections of the same WRP will enter Phases One, Two, and Three at different times in different localities. At any given stage a WRP may have units in Phase Three, Phase Two, and Phase One all interconnecting and providing propaganda and logistic support. When Phase Four comes, though, the entire WRP is affected.

The beginning of national-level Phase Two, however, will be marked by two key events. First off, a small national-level directorate or central command group will be formed, quite unofficially at first, based solely on functional considerations and merit. I'd use the term "Central Committee" if it didn't sound Marxist. These men and women will have no official titles or offices except empty ones giving them the authority to speak and negotiate with the enemy where absolutely necessary, such as "chairman" of a letterhead front group or editor of a photocopied newsletter. But everyone in the WRP's activity units will know that when Big Bob from down the road in Riverdale or wherever offers an opinion it's not an opinion, it's party policy.

The second keynote to Phase Two will be the initial issue of *a fighting publication* which will run through the entire revolution like a continuous, connecting thread or artery. This publication may start out as a mere photocopied "fanzine" type newsletter due to the perpetual financial shortages with which the revolutionaries will have to wrestle, but eventually it must become a tabloid newspaper — easy to fold and transport, the cheapest format to print and ship in bulk, the most word and graphic content for the money, the most psychologically authoritative presentation. There will be other organs in the WRP's underground press, to be sure, ideally ranging from crude pulp "hate-niggers" agitational material to slick and urbane theoretical journals. But the party organ itself must always constitute the prime agitprop weapon.

The circulation of the party newspaper must be the primary duty of each activist, and the distribution networks through which it gets into the hands of the White population will constitute ideal cells and channels for future political and extra-political activity. An entire covert organization that is no organization can be built around the distribution of an unapproved and eventually banned publication. In addition, the party organ will constitute the main conduit for the leadership to communicate ideas, policies, and directives to the base of support at the bottom of the pyramid, among the White population itself. For many of our isolated comrades way out in Grease Gap, Texas or Catamite Falls, Pennsylvania the party newspaper will be their only line of communication with the greater movement.

Phase Two will have three primary objectives for the WRP. If the party attempts to move into Phase Three prematurely, before these goals have been accomplished, then Phase Three will be the shortest and the terminal phase, because the WRP will be clobbered in very short order. The System is quite capable of recognizing a genuine threat to its power and its existence and will react.

The first Phase Two objective must be *to prepare the party to engage the enemy.* This means recruiting new people in the manner already described but also lining up finance; technical plant and necessary equipment for a political offensive; premises of safety where the WRP can work and store plant in some degree of security; making contacts with sympathetic personnel where we will need such contacts; intelligence preparation and the establishment of an information-gathering apparatus; research on the applicable enemy laws and regulations which they will use to harass and disrupt the WRP; establishment of a series of dummy corporations and other paper entities to transfer and hide assets from harassing private lawsuits, a favorite enemy weapon; selection of public spokesmen and the organization of activity units.

The second objective must be the most comprehensive and sustained *propaganda work among the White population* possible with the limited resources available to the WRP. The White people inhabiting each designated operational area must somehow be de-anesthetized and de-conditioned from the lifelong boob tube indoctrination they have been subjected to. They must be politically awakened and made racially aware, so that they will give tacit if not active support to the WRP. This is a tall order, true enough, and it is going to be a long hard task, but *it has to be done.* There is simply no way around it, no short cut. The WRP must establish its own channels of communication directly into the White community, bypassing and circumventing the enemy media. The White community in turn must learn to listen to what the WRP says and not the tube. This is going to take time, a lot of hard work, and a lot of empathy and grass roots understanding of the communities in which the WRP operates. But there simply isn't any other way.

By all means, let's take advantage of the technology our race has created and which the enemy is using to destroy us. Computers, videos, cassette tapes, CB radio, public access television, all of these are within our reach if we try. But nothing will ever beat good old face-to-face conversation with a real live human being instead of a Barbie doll feminist newscaster or a Max Headroom-type hologram. Our people will respond to the living human WRP activist in smaller numbers but to a greater degree than they obey their electronic programming. It can be done, my brothers. *It can be done!*

The third major project which must be undertaken during Phase Two, and the one I am looking forward to with the most pleasure and anticipation, is the initiation of *psychological warfare against the enemy.* The object of this campaign will be to soften up various governmental and private formations we will be fighting, in preparation for Phases Three and Four. The psywar the White revolutionaries undertake during Phase Two will be seemingly petty and minor at first, and it will be small beer compared to the later phases, but the WRP can develop its skills and techniques for later stages of the struggle.

Psychological warfare serves several vitally important purposes, and there is no reason at all for us to hold off on doing whatever we can to rattle the enemy's cage. Psywar unnerves the enemy, demoralizes him, confuses him about his own role in the scheme of things. Psywar misleads the enemy about our numbers, our intentions, our capabilities, and his own vulnerability. The phrase generally used to describe the desired effect of psywar is "alarm and despondency"; when the enemy is in that frame of mind, when he is nervous and uncertain, then he starts to make mistakes which rebound to our favor. Psychological warfare should make the enemy *doubt.* It should also raise our own morale correspondingly. It is vitally necessary for the *esprit de corps* and the resolution of the White revolutionary party that the White man should *strike back,* at least once in a while.

For various reasons I do not want to get into specific details here about psychological warfare. It is a complex and vital subject all on its own and needs to be studied and mastered as such. However, one of the more trenchant facts which have emerged over the past years of trial and error is just how *little* it takes to get the enemy hot under the collar, especially the Jews. It is entirely possible for a White revolutionary party to create total uproar and confusion in the agencies of government and blind hysterical panic among the Jews without breaking a single System "law" and spending very little money in the process. "The guilty flee where no man pursueth..." saith the immortal Bard of our race, and with all the hideous crimes against humanity that the Jews have on their collective conscience it is small wonder that they see Stormtroopers hidden behind every bush and SS men under the bed. "Holocaust" nonsense aside, that whole Third Reich episode brought the Chosen People a bit too close to the bar of justice for comfort, and they are quaking in their boots in fear of a repetition they might not be able to contain and destroy. Play on that fear, my brothers! Remember, an unnerved and rattled Jew is a Jew who makes mistakes.

Psychological warfare should be handled in the main by the national-level central directorate, but there is no reason why local activists should not try their hand. It is cost-effective, when properly used it is reasonably safe, and it plants seeds that will lead to unexpected harvests for many years into the future. Remember these basic principles: psywar should demoralize, confuse, and mislead the enemy while it encourages our own people and other Whites. Psywar should take advantage of our strengths, our anonymity, our moral rectitude, while zeroing in on the enemy's weaknesses such as his own uncertainty and his internal divisions. As soon as Phase Two begins is the time to start experimenting with various techniques and ideas along this line.

Enemy reaction to the WRP will begin in Phase Two. Ideally, the enemy should not have any idea that the WRP even exists during Phase One, and if they do detect the activity units during cadre recruitment then something has gone badly wrong. Either the WRP has not adhered to the strict security precautions that common sense dictates or else there is an informer about. However, when Phase Two begins and literature starts getting distributed, people start getting approached, and psychological warfare begins, then the cat will be out of the bag. If Phase One has been handled correctly, then the local ZOG in each locality selected as an operational area should be caught napping. Their nerves will be jarred by this, a psychological coup in itself for our side.

They will be surprised and may overreact with police raids, harassment arrests, defunctionalization of identified activists through job deprivation and prohibition of employment, and so on. Failing this reaction, and largely depending on how many Jews there are in the operational area and what kind of pressure they are exerting, the local police may decide to send in a low-level informer to take a look around and see if they can get an idea of the numbers and identities of those involved in the WRP. Careful recruiting should minimize this possibility. The informer will probably be a marginal character with a record of drugs or petty crime rather than a badge-carrying police officer, and someone like that has no business being recruited into the WRP. A word of warning: *watch out for women informers.* The first spy the Raleigh police department sent into the North Carolina NSPA in 1977 was a woman, a drug-user and a part-time prostitute who traded her services as a would-be Mata Hari for lenient treatment on a narcotics charge. I caught her out in time, but if we had been doing anything illegal she probably would have picked up on it and burned us.

Enemy attack: Legal and quasi-legal harassment in an attempt to arrest WRP activists and charge them with real or imagined "crimes".

White counter: Stay completely legal. Stay so clean you squeak. Don't jaywalk, don't spit on the sidewalk. As of this writing it is still possible to do this in the United States and to a certain extent in other countries. If they still want to proceed and try to can you, they will have to rely purely on fabricated evidence and paid perjury. They will probably be reluctant to do this during the early stages of the political struggle. Any prosecutor or police chief knows that fabricated evidence and perjured testimony can be very dicey. It can come unraveled even years after the conviction is secured and cause all manner of embarrassment. Later on they will not hesitate to fabricate or perjure, but *usually* not in the early stages unless they are under very strong pressure indeed from the local hebes.

Enemy attack: Planting *agents provocateur* in order to inveigle WRP activists into committing crimes so they can be interned under color of law.

White counter: Never let anyone join your group. Your group joins them. You select your potential recruits, screen their backgrounds, get to know them, examine their beliefs and attitudes, and finally bring them into the circle of activists. *Never let anyone volunteer* unless it is someone you know from childhood on a virtually blood-brother basis, and maybe not even then. Remember that gold can turn even the oldest friend to a stranger. Do not allow careless or loose talk of illegality. Be extremely suspicious of anyone who comes sniffing around offering you "deals" on guns, explosives, extremely cheap auto parts, whatever. *Stay functional. Stay on the street.* You do nobody any good whatsoever in jail.

Enemy attack. Media attention concentrating on identifying the WRP's members and targeting them for victimization. They will follow suspected WRP members to their jobs and harass fellow employees and supervisors with questions and TV cameras, thus ensuring the activist is fired in double-quick time. They will photograph a suspected racist's home and print the photo and address on the front page of their newspaper and negroidal papers as well, often actively inciting blacks to attack the man and his family. They will print photos of the known or suspected White activist and doctor the pictures to make him appear ugly, overweight, or exhibiting a bizarre facial expression. If allowed into a meeting or given an interview, they will write disparaging things about our people or their homes, twisting and distorting what we say to make us appear stupid or illiterate.

White counter. Avoid the media like the plague. Do not answer their questions. Do not give interviews. Refer them to the national or state level leadership whose job it will be to deal with the media during Phase Two. The state or national leadership should respond only to written questions, in writing, in carefully selected words and phrases to give the media as little to seize upon and distort as possible. Remember, with a reporter there is no such thing as "off the record." Also remember that all media representatives are the enemies of our race and should be treated accordingly. Insofar as possible, ignore the media completely. Concentrate on doing your job, which is to work within the White community itself and prepare for active engagement.

During Phase Two the activities of each local WRP cell or unit will be reported to the ADL office in one of the local synagogues. A file will be begun on activities and identifiable personnel in the area and all of this will be passed on to the national ADL headquarters who will in turn pass it on to the Israeli Mossad, which handles covert operations and terrorism for Zionist interests and world Jewry. Please bear in mind that any of our people who is identified by the enemy is quite likely to be murdered at some future stage when the Jews take the gloves off. Try to keep identification of members and supporters at an absolute minimum. Otherwise many of our people are going to die.

Many of us are already marked for eventual death in any case, because in previous years we attended silly little "rallies", open meetings where security was non-existent, allowed our license numbers to be taken down by the FBI or local police, allowed our photographs to be taken wearing 1930s uniforms or Klan robes, etc. All of that information is now in ZOG's computer banks and one day thousands of White patriots are going to be arrested, interned, tortured, and murdered because some asinine little jerk of a "mini-führer" wanted to go and scream in the streets and get his picture on the six o'clock news. With luck, many of us will be able to escape and evade the eventual Equality

Police dragnet, and fight on in the underground. But that does not mean that the policy of open public functions makes any more sense.

We are, in theory, committed to destroying this evil System. Why then do we courteously hand this deadly enemy our names, addresses, and occupations on a silver platter, in exchange for being allowed to parade in an absurd comic-opera uniform or a bedsheet? Because a good many of the people leading us in the past are criminal frauds or just plain idiots, that's why. One day we are going to hear that knock on the door, or more likely, we will hear our doors being kicked in at four in the morning as the secret police of Zionism and the Dollar Bill come to take us away. I sure hope those of us who won't make it looked good on the six o'clock news all those many years ago. Because we are going to pay long and hard for strutting our stuff in our regalia in our wild youth.

Some final general guidelines for Phase Two: work *directly in population,* keep your noses to the grindstone and concentrate on the job at hand, and ignore all potential diversions and distractions. *Do not engage the enemy directly* although you may wage hit-and-run raids on his psyche as best you can. Above all, *stay away from the media. You* can't stop them from printing garbage about you, but don't give them any help.

PHASE THREE:
Political and Propaganda Attack

In Phase Three, after presumably adequate preparation of the operational area during Phase Two, the White revolutionary party will begin actual attacks on the institutions and apparati of repression which ZOG uses to control and enslave the White race. The main guise the WRP will be forced to assume during this phase will be that of the legal political party, but there will be many others — labor unions for White workers, social clubs and societies, front groups, special-issue committees and movements, a whole underground White press and new White media system, "sports clubs" which in fact give military training, etc. The shape of the WRP must be fluid and easily malleable, because during this period the enemy will use their "law" to attempt to suppress White dissent using things like RICO, "civil rights" laws, private lawsuits, etc. The objective must be to *hit the enemy hard* and then dance back out of reach, so that his claw closes on empty air when he seeks to grip the WRP.

Every form of propaganda will be used during this phase — electoral politics; the underground press; "street theater" publicity stunts; graffiti; pirate radio; clandestine videos; computers; passive resistance and civil disobedience; infiltration of enemy formations; massive psychological warfare; economic and social sabotage of anti-White institutions and programs; deliberate disruption of enemy lines of supply and communication in order to cause confusion and overload his already decrepit infrastructure; and strong personal attacks against the enemy leadership to discredit and undermine the System's authority.

COMPREHENSION: Phase Three should consist of everything short of actual illegality and violence.

The enemy will counterattack, brutally and bloodily. Make no mistake: in Phase Three we are going to begin burying friends and comrades. We are going to suffer, but sooner or later we must stand up to ZOG and fight the monster hand to hand. We will never be able to sneak a victory out from under the enemy's nose. The White man has proven himself worthy of his destiny more than once in the past, at Tours when he fought back the crescent of Islam; at Wittenberg when Luther nailed the Ninety-Five Theses to the door of All Saints' Church and gave the Aryan back his God of Wrath; in the snows at Valley Forge; in the German beerhalls where the Jews' Marxism got its first defeat from the fists of the Stormtroopers. That destiny has now fallen upon us, the White racial nationalist revolutionaries of this generation and the next. We cannot evade it or shirk it. If we do, then our race will perish. We are going to have to *go mano a mano* with Yehudi and his mindless money-slaves, his computers, and his hordes of mud-colored humanoids. Even if somehow we could sneak and lie and finagle our way to victory, such is not the way of the men of the North.

I cannot sit here at my work table, tapping away at my little manual typewriter, and tell the whole world how it ought to be done. One day I will show you how I feel it should be done rather than tell you, but until that day comes I would simply be an armchair general if I were to tell you, my brothers, "First you do this during Phase Three, then you do that, then you do the other thing" Bear in mind that by now the revolution will have acquired a life of its own and the WRP's power to control events may be severely circumscribed. I am not so much describing a deliberate plan during the last two Phases as I am the natural evolution of an inevitable historic process. In Phase One and Phase Two, the WRP will be in charge of events, on top of things. (It had damned well *better* be, at any rate!) But my guess is that when the WRP makes the decision to move into open confrontation with the enemy, then the roller coaster ride begins and nobody gets off until it stops.

I have only one piece of urgent advice to offer for Phase Three: *stay legal. Stay functional. Stay on the street.* The pressure that the enemy brings against you will be enormous, my brothers, something we cannot now imagine. My one nightmare has always been that the White resistance will be pushed into making some doomed, premature military adventure and the timetable set back beyond recovery. Take the insults, take the harassment, if necessary take the casualties, the beatings, the murders, but stay on the street, my brothers. *Stay on the street!*

PHASE FOUR:
Armed Struggle Against Tyranny

Eventually, presuming the WRP plays all its cards right, the pressure on the System will simply be too much and it will fall back on its last resort: the open discard of the U.S. Constitution and straight martial law. The Bill of Rights will be officially a dead letter even as it now is in fact, Anyone suspected of the horrendous crime of "racism" will simply be hauled away in the night and locked up in a concentration camp or else murdered and dumped in a secret mass grave somewhere.

At this point, the ball game finally changes. At long last the masks of legality and fairness will be ripped from the faces of the Jew and his hirelings and there Yehudi will stand, dripping Talmudic hatred, screaming in his fear and rage, urging on his slaves to destroy the hated Aryan *goyishe* race. In his hysteria and his maniac lust for blood he will no longer have the desire or the capability to maintain the boob-tube anesthesia of the White populace and our millions of brothers and sisters will slowly begin to awaken. They will see the soldiers on America's streets, OD green uniforms with black and brown and yellow faces. All of a sudden, they will understand if they did not before, and then the miracle will occur.

The White population of America will withdraw its consent to be governed by ZOG. From then on, our victory is certain.

Most of them will never lift a finger to help us, of course, but neither will they hinder us. They will not report our presence to ZOG troops. When directly asked for assistance at least half of them will provide it, if a bit fearfully and grudgingly. The younger Whites will be more favorably inclined, and will provide intelligence and logistic support. White doctors will treat our casualties and say nothing to the soldiers. Other Whites will strike small individual blows, sugaring a bureaucrat's gas tank, wrongly programming computers, "losing" crucial tax records, minor industrial sabotage. Enemy troops searching for White guerrillas will be misdirected or led into guerrilla ambushes. Television crews will be sent on wild goose chases or suffer inexplicable losses of equipment, flat tires, acid poured onto film, etc.

In Phase Four we will reap the fruit of years and years of political organization and propaganda and hard work. Once we even enter that stage our victory is certain. By banning us and by "officially" suspending or revoking the Constitution the enemy will have admitted defeat. And if he could not hold us down with all his money, his computers, his television, and his Holocaust lie, then how can he keep us down with mere guns and barbed wire?

V.
THE ARMED STRUGGLE

At this point I believe it is necessary to clarify my own views on White political violence and on the role of armed struggle in the White resistance. I am going to have to choose my words rather carefully here, and for a time I considered writing this chapter in what Lenin termed "Aesopian language," that is to say, the language of fable, in order to evade harassment from the System's prosecutors and persecutors. However, I have decided not to attempt anything more or less than a direct statement of my genuinely held opinions.

For one thing, I don't want anyone to labor under any confusion as to precisely what I am trying to say here. The topic is an important one and clarity is essential. For another, by playing word games and trying to hedge and qualify, I am conceding to the enemy a very significant moral victory. ZOG does not *want* White men saying out loud the true and uncensored things we feel and know. In fact, the System goes to a good deal of trouble to force White racialists to wrap their beliefs in woolly language and cloak their true meanings in ritual disclaimer. They are unable as yet completely to ban all White racial nationalist speech and writing, although that draws closer very year. For the moment they content themselves with shutting off all meaningful access to the media of communications to our spokesmen while forcing those same spokesmen into double-talk and allegorical language through fear of malicious private lawsuits, "sedition" laws, "incitement to racial hatred" local ordinances, all the niggling little tactics they use to salami-slice our rights away, thin layer by thin layer.

But this is a book for the instruction of White racial nationalist revolutionaries, and for once my brothers and sisters shall hear spoken aloud the truths that many of our so-called "leaders" fear to utter, and which ZOG definitely does not want you to think about.

First off, do I, Harold A. Covington, advocate violence? No, I do not. Do I advocate the forcible overthrow of the United States government? Not in the sense of "Hey, let's all get guns and march on Washington and kill all the politicians!", I don't. What do I advocate? I advocate the survival of the White, Aryan race of human beings. All right then, *how* do I advocate the White race should go about insuring its survival? At this point I can envision a team of ADL and Justice Department lawyers poring over this chapter with a fine toothed comb, quietly begging me "Please oh please, Harold, be a good little Nazi and say something we can arrest you for! Please, chust *vun* liddle bit of sedition or treason? Maybe a few words we can make a conspiracy case on? Chust a *liddle* bit incitement violence mebbe? Anything at all ve can come and lock you up wit', hokay?"

Guys, it's like this. I don't advocate anything. I don't *incite* to anything. I don't have to. I have studied the history of this insane world and the equally insane human species that inhabits it, and I don't have to incite my White brothers and sisters to do anything that might violate your precious goddamned "law." What is going to happen to this country, what is going to happen throughout the world over the next century or so, is the inevitable result of the policies that world Zionism and its allies have followed since about 1890, before that if you want to get esoteric. What is going to happen to all you wretched little Jews out there has nothing to do with anything that I may write here, or that George Lincoln Rockwell wrote in 1960, or Adolf Hitler wrote in 1924. The coming destruction of Jewry and all its unclean works is the logical and natural conclusion of the behavior of the Jewish people. Whether or not you silence me or a thousand like me is immaterial. We are not instigators, we are simply commentators and, in a few cases, we are prophets. We are not bringing upon you Jews the doom that you see approaching. You have brought it on yourselves through your own behavior.

I do not advocate violence. I do not incite violence. I personally do not want to see violence. I *have* seen it in the past. I find it squalid, distasteful and sickening. I have served in two armies and two wars and I have experienced all manner of politically motivated and racially rooted violence. I know what bullets, bombs, shrapnel, knives, broken bottles, and blunt instruments do to the human body because I have seen it. I am not sitting here pontificating about something I know only from the flicks and dry pages of books. I have lived in Ireland and 1 have seen what sustained political paramilitary violence does to the fabric of society, aside from the actual bloodshed itself. I would never willingly unleash such events on my own country.

And yet, when the only alternative is craven submission, abject surrender, and acceptance of our own deaths, what choice is that? If the

Jews didn't want to risk violence at the hands of the Aryan, they should not have behaved in the manner they have over the decades and the centuries. The violence which has been directed against them and their hirelings, and which will be directed against them and their hirelings in the future, is the foregone and inevitable result of the policies which the Jewish people themselves and their Zionist Occupational Governments have pursued for at least three generations.

I do not incite. I merely predict. If my predictions are accurate, then it is not my fault, but the fault of those whose behavior will have brought destruction on themselves.

Whether human nature is the slave of historical imperative, or whether it's the other way around, I have yet to figure out. All I know is that throughout the ages human beings have invariably reacted in the same way to similar sets of circumstances. The simple fact is that *you can push people only so far* before they react violently to such things as oppression, assault, robbery, slander, systematic murder of their friends and family, mass rape of their women, in short, all the little peccadilloes that American society foists on the White man. White Americans do not need to be lectured about the evils of violence. They live with it every day. The level of daily intimidation and anxiety that Whites must deal with in their enforced relations with non-Whites is gargantuan in scope. The number of White women over the past thirty years who have been raped, sexually humiliated, and mentally scarred for life by non-Whites is beyond the power of the human mind to comprehend or the pen to relate. The agonizing terror that elderly Whites undergo, trapped by fixed incomes in non-White neighborhoods, is an appalling disgrace to whatever is left of our racial manhood.

White Americans are the daily victims of *institutional violence* and aggression from non-Whites. This institutional violence is not only condoned but deliberately instigated and orchestrated by the Federal government of the United States. The Black Terror serves a number of purposes from ZOG's point of view. It rewards negroids and Hispanics for their support of the System. It terrorizes Whites into a pattern of submissive behavior and conditions them into a reflexive fear and panic reaction. It helps to suppress White political dissent, because White Americans know that if they dare to voice any kind of protest that means anything they will be victimized by non-White violence and nothing will be done about it. White fear and suffering is played on by the System for a variety of purposes, to manipulate White votes, to channel White anger and frustration into "acceptable channels" (i.e., dead ends), and to wage psychological warfare against the White community as a whole. The police do occasionally apprehend, and the courts do occasionally imprison, the more blatant negroidal and Hispanic hoodlums, but this is only for the purpose of maintaining the minimum of order and safety necessary to ensure continued production by White workers. Prison is no deterrent to negroids or spics who consider their sentences to be a sort of vacation where they can hang out in the yard with all their "home boys" and watch color TV all day.

The ultimate aim of all this incalculable daily violence and intimidation is, of course, the genocide of the White race. Black and brown violence is the cutting edge of the enemy strategy, a sort of ongoing mass murder which we have become accustomed to and which we accept with all the uncaring apathy of hogs awaiting to be slaughtered. The horrific general orgy of rape inflicted on White women compensates for the (to ZOG) unacceptably low rate of voluntary miscegenation among Aryan females. The orphanages and reformatories of America are filled to capacity today with half-breed children who are by and large the product of black/brown-on-White rape. These half-breeds will grow up to repeat the process, the males becoming rapists themselves and the females going on welfare and producing large numbers of piccaninnies.

COMPREHENSION White Americans have every moral right to resist the Federal government of the United States by any means necessary, including by force of arms, in order to prevent further implementation of that government's genocidal policies.

The moral choice facing the White man in America is simple: pick up a gun and fight, or die. It is the age old moral quandary of dying on one's feet as opposed to living on one's knees. So far, I am ashamed to say, my people have chosen to live on their knees. But that does not mean that they will always so choose. I would hope that eventually they will awaken and arise. Indeed, I am personally convinced that they will. The only question is whether or not they will awaken in time.

The *moral* issues are quite clear cut and 100 per cent in favor of open and armed revolt against Washington and the filthy hordes of Jewry. However, we live in a real world and our choices must be based on reality if we are to have any hope of surviving. Just because Whites are morally entitled to revolt does not mean that it would be wise for them to do so now, or at any time in the foreseeable future. In point of fact, organized armed violence against ZOG is not practicable nor will it be any time soon. The Movement is not prepared militarily and our people as a whole are not prepared politically and emotionally for any kind of physical strike against the System. White racial nationalists must refrain from acts of violence and illegality, not because it would be wrong to attack a genocidal régime, but because *we cannot win.* When it comes to the survival of the White race, failure is the only immorality, and destroying our chances of victory through a premature military campaign would be just as bad as failure ever to strike a blow in our defense.

COMPREHENSION: We must not undertake any armed revolt or guerrilla campaign until, by the best possible calculation and extrapolations, we have at least a 50/50 chance of victory.

I myself am just not prepared to risk losing everything we've worked for over two generations on a throw of the military dice unless we've got at least a 50/50 chance, and no other White racial nationalist should be either. How do we gauge the odds? When we can be as sure as we possibly can that it will be *our 5%* of the White population against *their 5%* of the population and the remaining 90% of the White community will either remain neutral or be passively tilted towards our side. In other words, they won't help us actively but *they won't help the government forces either.* That's the best we can do. Knock out the passive support of he people from under the régime and leave them with their computers, their Yuppies, their paid mercenaries, and their niggers; given proper preparation on our side, we'll take on Uncle and wipe the sidewalk with him and his pals. Because we're better than they are.

In Phases One, Two, and Three the watchword must be *stay straight!* Stay so clean you squeak! Stay functional, and stay on the street! I know I've said this all before, but it bears repeating. If you as a revolutionary allow yourself to get locked up doing a fifty-year sentence in some hellhole prison, you aren't worth a tinker's damn to yourself or anybody else. In these early phases there is no *need* to break the law. There is still so much we can do within the parameters of Big Brother's "legality" if we will just use our imaginations and try new tactics, new methods, never hitting him where he expects us and then never letting him get a grip on us. There is nothing that Big Brother likes better than to have a "handle" on a White revolutionary — some Mickey Mouse charge that he can use to keep us on bail, on remand, bouncing in and out of his courtrooms, on probation, under court order to avoid "improper associations" (i.e., other White racialists), and so forth and so on. *Don't give Big Brother a handle on you!*

I fully understand the frustration, the anger, the depression, the despair that grips our people as they slog on and endlessly on, year after year, never seeing any progress, isolated and alienated and broke and their nerves worn to fiddle strings by the constant pressure of living outside the comfortable herd. I understand the longing to pick up a shotgun and erase the gibbering black and brown faces that surround you, to silence those horrible negroidal booga-booga-booga voices that drive you mad with their sheer glutinous ugliness. I understand the longing to *make something happen,* anything, even if it is at the cost of your own life. My brothers and sisters, I beg of you not to yield to that temptation. Your lives are precious to me and they are precious to us all. Your lives are jewels granted unto you by Almighty God and not to be thrown down into the mud without hope, without purpose. So what if you kill a few token congoids or even a few Jews? They are breeding faster than you could possibly kill them, and they are not worth one drop of your crystalline Aryan blood.

Our objective is not to achieve private revenge or satisfaction for the injuries that we have suffered as individuals. Our purpose is not even to avenge our race as a whole, although during the course of our work we will partially obtain just such a generic vindication. Our objective is to *change the world.* The greatest monument we can offer to our brothers and sisters who have died and who have suffered is to ensure that our children and theirs can walk in the sunlight instead of the dark night of Zion. White victory will be the sweetest revenge of all.

COMPREHENSION: Despite the present necessity of strict legality, all white revolutionaries must understand that eventually there will be an armed confrontation with the United States government.

Such a confrontation will occur as a matter of historic inevitability, and it will be the Federal government which initiates armed warfare when we are defeating it politically. This is the beginning of Phase Four.

We must all accept that eventually there will come the knock on the door in the dark of night, or more likely the crash of our doors splintering open at four in the morning as ZOG's secret police come to take us away. Eventually we are going to find the right track politically and propaganda-wise and we are going to press the System so hard that it must take the final, decisive step of throwing away its own Constitution. Pressure on the establishment will become so great that mere salami tactics, the gradual slicing away of our rights, will no longer suffice. Then will come the "emergency" legislation, the internment camps, the barbed wire, the torture chambers, the secret trials and summary executions, the mass roundups of Whites, the Equality Police to suppress all manifestations of "racism," all the panopoly of tyranny and genocide. Whites will then have no choice any longer. They can take up the gun or they can die. Some will choose to die, but more will fight. Remember, always remember those Viking chromosomes!

The whole trick to our successful revolution must be to *hold off the final confrontation as long as possible.* Every year we get a little stronger and they get a little weaker, and since there is no conceivable way in which the present Establishment can right itself and correct conditions in this country, time can only be on our side. Every year more Whites are brutalized and alienated, every year the System weakens and its arteries harden a little more, every year the odds inch upwards in our favor by a tiny fraction of a percentage point. When the fight does come we will be a numerical minority, another bad aspect we are going to have to accept, because the bulk of our people simply won't be willing to wake up out of their boob-tubular slumber until that happens. We are going to lose God alone knows how many brothers and sisters to the Black Terror, to rape and intimidation, to the System's hellish prisons. We are going to have to swallow untold abuse, humiliation, insult, and degradation ourselves, waiting for the proper time to strike. But that time will come, my brother! That magical 50/50 will come, and then the streets will run red with the filthy blood of Yehudi and his hirelings and his mud-colored pets! Work for that day, my brothers. *Work* for it, and above all, *live* for it! Don't let Big Brother take you out now, or else you'll miss that great day.

For now, when the Jew's law says frog, we jump. When the law says jump, we say "how high?" When the law says run, we say "how far?" I wish there was another way, my brothers. But there isn't.

VI.
THE TRICKS OF THE TRADE

Pay close attention to this chapter, brothers, because it will save you from wasting a lot of time in a lot of dead ends. It will teach you the useful short cuts you need to know and it will teach you the things you can't afford to take short cuts on. I'm going to pass on to you some tactical tidbits that may seem simple, obvious, or in some cases unnecessary and outdated. Feel free to adapt and improve on them, but remember that some of these little skills and tactics we have learned over the years through bitter experience. Some of the knowledge here has been literally bought with White blood, so even if you don't fully appreciate it now, don't despise it.

The first thing you will need is reasonably secure communications, as inexpensively as possible. In actual practice, this means a very heavy reliance on the mail. The present postage rate is 22 cents per inland letter, and that's not cheap, but compared to three minutes of telephonic communications at even the lowest rate it's value for money. You will need at least one public access address, such as a post office box or an absolutely secure street address, for incoming mail from the public and for your official address of record. You should also have at least two or three secure mail drop addresses, unknown to the enemy, where you can receive mail safely and confidentially.

The primary enemy technique for surveilling your mail is what is called the "mail cover." This involves scrutiny of your incoming, and in some case your outgoing mail in every way short of actually opening it. They note postmarks, return addresses, any possible ways of identifying the sender or the contents. Sometimes this is done by postal employees and sometimes by FBI agents or local cops. I used to look through the little glass windows at the central Raleigh post office in the mornings and watch our Jewish Special Agent-in-Charge of the "Nazi desk" going over Party mail with the negroidal postal clerks, trying to figure out who was writing to us and why. On several occasions I opened the post office box with my key, so they could hear me, and called out various jibes such as, "That's a letter from my girl friend!" or "I've been waiting for that one, it's from the ACLU," or else just "Would you guys hurry up? I want to get my mail and go to breakfast!" We Were Not Amused.

A mail cover is technically supposed to be done only with a court order but the enemy ignores that at his pleasure just like he ignores most other such regulatory incunabulae. Rules are for us sharecropping peasants and the law is not only an ass, it is a three-ringed circus with a cageful of baboons. They aren't supposed to open your mail except with a court order for each individual item in relation to specific charges and looking for certain specific evidence, just like searching your home requires a warrant. This is another one you can tell to the Marines. I can't count how many letters and parcels the NSPA received over the years "opened by mistake." One parcel arrived at our Chicago headquarters showing visible *teeth marks,* where some nigger in the post office had actually chewed the damned thing open and removed half the contents, whether under Federal direction or simply stealing, we never figured out.

In fact, they no longer need to open our mail covertly. The FBI, BATF, and other agencies now nave a flouroscoping device that enables them to X-ray your letters, then feed the resultant negative into a computer de-scrambling device which turns the thing into a kind of hologram, *unfolds the pages,* correlates all the data from the scan viz., paper thickness, ink density, you name it, and *reconstructs your letter in a hard copy form without ever actually opening the envelope!* The SOBs can actually read your mail without opening it! I used to laugh at people who enclosed their mail in aluminum or lead foil for fear of such scanning devices. Looks like the last laugh in that case is on me and not on those I once considered paranoid "kooks." Recently I've even been known to lead-wrap an especially sensitive letter or two myself, and if you're sending anything by post you don't want Big Brother to read, then don't hesitate to do this yourself.

One word of advice, though: when dealing with the American postal service, it is always a bit difficult to tell when you're confronted with deliberate tampering or whether it's simple nigger incompetence. The post office has traditionally been one of the major boondoggles for handing niggers Federal checks under the pretense that they are earning them, as well as a dumping ground for every White fool and malcontent who has wormed his way to the far bottom end of the public trough. The prime example of this came in 1979 when the JDL sent six parcel bombs to various NS groups and elderly Eastern Europeans, myself on the list. Five of the bombs arrived on schedule, were easily detected due to their clumsy construction and appearance, and were detonated by local bomb squads. Mine never arrived. *Those damned niggers in the post office lost my bomb!* For all I know, it may be sitting in the dead letter office in St. Louis or Saskatoon to this day. Or else some postal monkoid stole it, took it home to Frogtown thinking it was something good to eat, and got one hell of a surprise when he opened it.

I might add, to quell the levity here, that one of the recipients of these bombs was Tscherim Soobzokov, the Circassian community leader in New Jersey who was later murdered by the Jewish Defense League. Just a reminder that none of this is funny.

Telephones can be very useful tools of communication, but they tend to be expensive if used extensively and they also are susceptible to enemy harassment. I used to have to go over every Party phone bill removing all the JDL calls that had been billed to our number, Candygrams sent to strangers, phony telegrams billed to our number etc. Some Movement activists will disagree strongly with me on this point, but personally I see very little need for a White revolutionary party to have a publicly accessible telephone number. When you have a listed phone number, idiots call you and waste your time. I can't count how many hours I've wasted on the telephone in Arlington and in Raleigh on the pointless pursuit of trying to convince people to join us through reason. Reason has nothing to do with it; I doubt if I have ever persuaded one single White person to join the Movement through rational, logical reasoning during all the time I've been politically active. People will join us when they're sufficiently fed up with conditions beyond their control or ours. In the meantime, if you let them, they will call you on the telephone and talk cobblers for hours on end.

Another problem with an openly listed telephone number is the perpetual crank calls and hecklers who ring up. At first I used to enjoy sparring with these jerks, Jews and Feds and silly kids and occasional niggers, plus the Jesus Freaks and the sex perverts and the weirdos who wanted to tell me all about the green men from Planet Omega who were beaming bad vibes at their house. Eventually I figured out that tying up the Party telephone, even for a short time per each call, was a victory for them of sorts. While the White activist is diddling with some hebe heckler he might miss the crucial call warning of an impending police raid. The telephone is not a toy, it is a medium of communication and needs to be used, not played with.

A final word on using the telephone: *always, ALWAYS assume that your line is tapped!* In point of fact, it quite probably is tapped by at least one government agency and maybe several "private" ones like the ADL. It is true that if they want to use anything they record against you in court they have to have a court order, but that's a mere bureaucratic detail. They listen anyway, and if they pick up anything they think they can use to hang you with they just go to a sympathetic Federal judge and get him to sign a conveniently back-dated authorization. I repeat, *treat all telephones you use as if they were tapped!* Because it's very likely that they are.

LIFE IN THE TWILIGHT ZONE

As a White revolutionary you will find that you are living in a sort of limbo or Phantom Zone, You must live and function within so-called "normal" society and yet you are not, can never be, a part of that society. You can't re-join the herd even if you want to, because your brain has been disconnected from the goggle box and you can never be re-programmed. The Jews know this, and that is why they never forgive and never forget. There have been many cases I know of where activists have gotten fed up and tried to re-integrate themselves into what passes for "normality." They break off all political contacts, move to new cities, acquire a new circle of friends, even change their names sometimes. It never quite works out, not completely, and sometimes ten or fifteen years later the refugee will return to White racial nationalist activism.

The problem, the insurmountable obstacle, is that no matter how hard you try to conceal or forget the fact, *you KNOW!* You *know* about the Jews. You *know* what's going on and why things are as they are, and you can never pick up a newspaper or turn on the boob tube or walk down a city street again without interpreting everything you see, hear, and learn in the light of that knowledge. It doesn't matter whether your orientation was or is National Socialist, Identity, Klan, Revisionist, neo-Fascist, pagan revival, Posse Comitatus, what have you. The minute that spark of knowledge sputtered and flickered into a flame in your mind all those years ago, you were permanently and irrevocably lost to the soulless, glittering Eden of the Jews. Like Adam, you somehow were enticed to eat of the forbidden fruit and you can never again re-enter the false paradise of blissful ignorance, of taking everything at face value and *not knowing.* For some, the awareness that they can never go back even if they try is the worst thing about being involved.

The fact that you possess this precious knowledge and you must live and move in a community comprised mostly of people who do not is a very hard thing to adjust to and in the long run probably causes the most problems for the activist's psyche. The urgency of sharing the knowledge grips us all. We want to grab those dumb *goyim* by the lapels and scream in their faces and *shake* the knowledge into them, scream and shake until they understand. But we can't do that. We mustn't try. The fact is that the huge majority of our neighbors, acquaintances, and co-workers are not ready to assimilate this terrible knowledge and probably never will be. The only thing we will ever be able to do with most of them is persuade them, through the carrot or the stick or both, to withdraw their active coöperation with the régime and most of their passive cooperation as well. They will never help us, and we must be satisfied with their not helping ZOG either.

There is always a danger that we will overreact, that we will thereby get a reputation among our fellow Whites as being cranks, extremists, a bit "kooky." This is fatal to our credibility and must be avoided at all costs. The first step in communicating with people is to make them listen to what you have to say, because they believe it to be worth hearing. This means they must respect you as a person. If they respect you and like you as a man or a woman, then they will accord your political and social views that credence. People will not listen to "kooks." They will listen to other people whom they know through personal experience to be intelligent, of good character, mentally and sexually normal, not addicted to drugs or alcohol, responsible members of the community, and so on. This is the image we have to project, and our whole lives in the community must assist this end.

COMPREHENSION: White revolutionaries are always on stage. They cannot afford a single slip, not even the minor slips that the members of the White "audience" can get away with. The audience are not watching one another, they are watching YOU. Make sure they see a masterful performance.

Another problem White revolutionaries confront in their daily struggle is that of paranoia. The problem is that just because you're paranoid don't mean they ain't out to get you. They *are* out to get you.

Even paranoids have enemies, The trick is to distinguish between justifiable security precautions and baseless fears that can and sometimes do drive our people around the twist. It's a fine art, one you must learn through experience. I'll try to give you a few pointers, though.

First off, be familiar with those in your locality who may well actually try to do you harm. Develop a genuine intelligence system for your activity unit. Identify known JDLers or Communists, known undercover police and FBI, their vehicles and license numbers, their likely tactics and avenues of attack. Don't just sit and jump at shadows. The unknown is always unnerving, so try to make your genuine potential problems a known factor instead of an unknown one. Once you feel you have a fairly accurate idea of just what type of harassment you can expect (generally proportionate to your degree of activity), then try not to worry unduly. Take it all in stride. Assume your phones are tapped, but don't make a big production out of it. As far as possible, anticipate their moves and when they happen you won't go all spastic and discombobulated.

Yuppie executives and bureaucrats are constantly being warned about the dangers of stress, and that goes triple for White political activists. Your public image should be four-square and spit-shined and on the ball, but don't be afraid to pace yourself. Let your mind mellow out, relax periodically, get out of your city or wherever and get a change of scenery, somewhere close to nature, where you can hear the ocean and listen to the wind rustling the leaves on the trees. Invest in a good tape deck and unwind with good solid Aryan music, Baroque chamber ensembles or Hank Williams, whatever you feel best with. Play sports, rather than watch them on the boob tube. Play a musical instrument if you've the bent for it. Play chess, grow a garden. Don't let the pressure and the enemy's psychological warfare reduce you to a nervous wreck. *We* do that to *him.*

Before you get all paranoid about some minor incident, examine the physical evidence. You think your car has been tampered with? What concrete evidence is there? You think someone's been quietly rifling your home looking for "evidence," or planting same? What tangible evidence do you have for this belief? There is ample indication that enemy covert operations are generally pretty incompetent, and if they've been messing around they will generally leave some physical traces. If you can find no definite, tangible traces of enemy activity, then the chances are it's your overactive imagination.

Think! Always. Before you act, before you speak, *think!* That is the message of this book. Because the enemy very seldom does. The whole trick to pulling this off is to make the enemy *react* instead of acting, make him lash out in all directions, dissipate his efforts, attenuate his own strength in costly yet pointless dead ends. We can do this if we keep cool, keep our heads, *think,* plan ahead, and don't let him get us rattled. While, of course, we are simultaneously rattling the hell out of ZOG's cage. Paranoia is a weapon, a two-edged one. We must aim its cutting edge at the System while shielding ourselves against it. It's not easy, and it won't get any easier from now on, but it's a vitally important "trick of the trade" that we must all master.

HANDLING ENEMY SURVEILLANCE

The degree to which you will be harassed by the enemy's governmental agencies depends on two factors, the first being how active you are and how effective this activity is. The second related factor is the level of pressure that the local Jewish establishment and their non-White counterparts exert on the authorities to "do something about these horrible racist anti-Semites." Some local police departments are more politicized than others and are thus more susceptible to manipulation and coercion. Representations from the Anti-Defamation League of B'nai B'rith to take "an aggressive and creative law-enforcement stance" against White political dissent are more likely to influence the police in Silver Springs, Maryland than they are in Bugtussel, Mississippi. Not that the ADL can't get to the sheriff in Bugtussel as well, but it will take more time and they will have to do it more subtly, say through discreetly offered campaign contributions or else a quiet chat with the Mississippi governor in the State House over a bourbon and branch. You should familiarize yourself with precisely how ZOG operates in your locality and try to anticipate their moves.

One of the first things that the law will do is place any identifiable White racial nationalists under surveillance. This will vary in intensity and scope according to how much manpower is available, how strong the Jewish pressure is, and whether or not they really suspect you of doing anything illegal. (I repeat for the tenth time that during the first three phases of the revolutionary scenario you should stay squeaky clean.) Most White local police officers have more than enough genuine crime on their hands without wasting overmuch time and effort on surveilling legal political activists of their own race whom they probably agree with in secret, just to please the back-room boys downtown who are getting heat from Rabbi Shlumpfelstein of the Interfaith Human Relations Council or whatever the local ADL front is called.

If you can cultivate a good relationship with the low-ranking cops on the beat, this will pay immense dividends. In most departments, anyone from the rank of sergeant on up is politicized and eventually compromised by having to toe the line for ZOG and demonstrate "sensitivity to minority concerns," i.e., political reliability. But the cop on the beat gets the brunt of niggerism every day and he knows what's what. The mentality of the police will be discussed more fully later on, but here we are discussing dealing with them on a one-to-one street basis. Bear in mind that if and when you become sufficiently dangerous to the System to merit a violent assault on your life or your freedom, it is more than likely the cop on the beat, a White man like yourself, who will be sent after you. FBI and BATF have become somewhat antsy over the years about taking on White racialists and seldom do so anymore without extensive help from local police who will take the bulk of the risk if any shooting starts. (Local cops generally resent and despise Federal agents, something we can learn to play upon.)

Remember- a police officer is used to dealing with criminals and punks. Cheap bravado, obscene abuse, facile lies, sullen insolence, he's seen it all. If you behave in such a manner towards him, he will assume the rabbi is right and you're just low-life criminal scum, and he will treat you accordingly. Always treat White patrolmen and sergeants with respect, courtesy, and professionalism. This will pay dividends and besides, most of them deserve it. From lieutenant on upwards the rot starts setting in and the chances are very good you're dealing with a mercenary whose idea of loyalty is staying bought, even if his paymasters are engaged in destroying his race. With higher-ranking cops be cool, courteous, and correct. Tell them nothing whatsoever. Not ever, not under any circumstances. Do not discuss anything political with them at all. They are *not* potential recruits, they do nothing without a reason, and they are always after something out of you for their own nefarious purposes, (See the later chapter entitled *What to Do When You are Captured*.)

Electronic surveillance will be the most common form of spying that you will be subjected to. It is cost-efficient, relatively easy, and releases manpower for real criminal investigations. It enables the police to assure Rabbi Shlumpfelstein and City Councilman Nicodemus Washington that something really is being done about these horrible stroppy honkies and eventually they will be cast into the deepest and darkest dungeons of Zion where such heretics and blasphemers belong. In addition, if you are stupid enough to disregard my repeated injunctions against illegality, they may even catch you doing something unlawful and *really* lock you up. Technically all electronic surveillance is supposed to be strictly controlled and done only on foot of a court order but they can sanitize and legalize their tapes any time they want with the signature of a judge who will conveniently fail to notice that the documents are dated three months before. I have yet to hear of one single case where any police officer or Federal agent has been disciplined in any way for abusing electronic eavesdropping procedures. It is their main weapon against us, followed closely by the use of informers.

I have already discussed telephone tapping. It used to be they had to sneak into your home some way and actually install the bug inside the telephone receiver itself, but they do it all down at the switchboard now or else they tap into a line at a junction box on a pole some ways from your house or apartment. Chances are that when you move into a new neighborhood or get a new phone installed, and they find out about it, you will notice a phone company service van and a "lineman" up a pole nearby very shortly afterwards. It is therefore a good idea not to let them know which phones you are using for your political work. This isn't always easy, as their computers can take a list of known White patriots' phones countrywide, search your city or county's phone bills scanning hundreds of thousands of calls, and in a matter of minutes spit out a list of who in your area has been calling identified White racial nationalists. A rotating system of specific times and phone booths is better, but once again if they catch on they can use their computers to partially or wholly reconstruct your pattern of pay phone use and tap into the right lines at the right time.

Many phone taps simply have live recorders attached to them which are sound-sensitized to switch on and begin recording on certain key words such as "gun," "bomb," "kill," "Jew," etc. When you must speak on a tapped line, it might be a good idea to use Aesopian language, the language of fable. Use code words like "biscuit" for gun, "cement" for explosives, "cockroach" for Jew, etc. This presupposes that you are discussing such things on a tapped line to begin with, which isn't a good idea, but there are times when you must use these words in a wholly legitimate context. Many is the time in the NSPA when I said "guns" or "bombs' in a completely legal conversation, talking about some news item or article I was writing, and I heard an audible click as the recorder kicked in.

Actual bugs are often placed in the homes and the cars of White patriots, generally through "black bag jobs." These are burglaries conducted by police or Federal agents in order to conduct illegal searches, steal your property, plant electronic eavesdropping devices, or conceal incriminating evidence such as drugs or hand grenades in your home that they can then "find" on some pretext. There is really very little we can do about this if they are really determined, just stay legal, conduct periodic searches for the bugs, and drive on. If they want to put you away, they're going to do it and they won't allow picky little details like law, morality, or facts stand in their way. This is something we have to accept before we ever become involved in unapproved political activity. There are manuals available in the underground press on how to locate and remove bugging devices, how to do a "sweep," etc. Learn these techniques and practice them regularly. Be careful whom you talk to about what, be careful what you say on the phone, and keep on truckin'. I used to play games with surveillance teams. In Arlington sometimes I'd call out to the FBI shadow cars, "we going to the printers now!" or wherever we were going. Sometimes I'd lose them by running a red light, swinging around the block, and then pull up beside the baffled G-men at the next light and say, "Hi, guys! Nice weather we're having!" However, I forgot that this is not a game and these were vicious thugs I was messing with, and in due course I got my comeuppance.

I and one other smart-aleck kid at the NSWPP HQ decided to play a joke on the 'droids. We conducted an ostentatious conversation on the telephone about a shipment of illegal weapons, naming a place and time we were going to bury these items. We showed up with a couple of plastic bags full of dirty laundry and started digging, whereupon an army of flak-jacketed Feebies and local cops arose out of the earth and grabbed us. When it dawned on the pin-headed bastards that they had been the victim of a Dick Tuck prank, they took us into the District (we had been taken prisoner in Virginia) and locked us up in the Anacostia police station, a local D.C. copshop. We were never formally arrested during the entire 8-hour procedure. I was chained to a radiator and after a couple of hours a nigger D.C. police sergeant comes in and without a word proceeds to beat me within an inch of my life using a wet towel, his fists, and the open palms of his hands which he clapped together over my ears, damned near bursting my eardrums. The other kid got a similar treatment in the next room, from a White renegade cop. We were then kicked out the door of the police station and told to walk home to Arlington, this being about midnight in the worst nigger slum in Washington D.C.

The other kid couldn't take it and he left the HQ shortly afterwards. I stuck with the Movement but learned not to treat this struggle as a game. You'd better learn that too, brothers, and that right speedily. Your life may well depend on it. FBI men and other Federal agents especially are trained killers and in many cases the individuals you will be dealing with are actual murderers as well. We're damned lucky they didn't waste us and dump us in the Potomac that night. If they did, no one would have raised a whimper of protest, because we were "Nazis," and everybody knows" Nazis" have no right even to exist.

COMPREHENSION: It is unwise to play games with the secret police of any nation or government. Such men are not noted for their mellow natures or their sense of humor.

HOW TO SPOT AN INFORMANT

The second line of attack the enemy will use against your activity unit, eventually, will be the informer. It is important to realize that, owing to the nature of their function and their assignment within the activity unit, informers *always behave in the same way.* There are variations on the theme, but with a little percipience and a little savvy you will be able to spot the pattern. I repeat that virtually every agent or informer leaves the same telltale signs and detritus. I do not except the wretched Bernard Butkovich, the BATF agent who was instrumental in creating the Greensboro fiasco. We had, in fact, already spotted Butkovich as a plant and the last time he showed up at a Party meeting we were only constrained by the presence of reporters and TV cameras from confronting him with the evidence we had gathered. Butkovich was only unusual in that he was an actual badge-carrying ATF agent, whereas most informers are a lower type of criminal, a petty thief or drug user.

I might add that Butkovich's subsequent death in a mysterious plane crash provides an interesting little moral for those 'droids in three-piece suits who trust in Uncle Slime as the Great White Father who will forever cherish and protect them in his worm-ridden bosom. Butkovich embarrassed Uncle with his incompetence, and Uncle doesn't appreciate being embarrassed by his servants. And an awful lot of things can go wrong with those little private planes, even for an experienced pilot .... ah, but I digress. *RI.P.,* scumbag.

The following points are to be looked for in various plants. They may not all be present, but look for an *overall pattern* of suspicious behavior and odd coincidences. Also, certain patterns of behavior and activity indicate that you may be dealing with an actual Fed or other gumshoe-type cop.

1. *Petty criminal activity.* Most informers indulge in some type of penny-ante crime, ripping off vending machines, selling or using soft drugs, "five finger discounts" at the K-mart or the grocery store, etc. People like that shouldn't be in your White political activity unit in any case, but I mention this because it is an important indicator of *attitude.* Someone who will shoplift or steal from a parked car or sell drugs has no personal sense of integrity or honor and will sell out you, his friends, his own grandmother or whomever in exchange for small amounts of money, or else immunity from prosecution. The most pathetic case I ever heard of was the Royal Canadian Mounted Police's prime informant in a number of Assorted Canadian groups. For years, this man's price was ten Canadian dollars and *two bottles of rum* every week. I don't know which is more grotesque, that or the fact that the man is still hanging onto the periphery of the Movement despite his record and his obvious alcoholism and senility.

2. *The informer talks big but produces little.* He's always around, always wanting to meet new people, always wanting to sponge off any freebies going, always full of stories about how he's going to do this, that, and the other thing for the Movement. And yet somehow, these great things never seem to materialize. The late Joe Tommasi was warned by a contact at local police HQ that such a low-life was attempting to infiltrate his NSWPP unit in Los Angeles on behalf of the LAPD. Tommasi applied a simple remedy: every time the guy came around the El Monte headquarters he was put to work, and dirty work at that. He washed dishes; he cleaned the printing press; he mowed the lawn; he folded newspapers until his fingers were black with ink; he cleaned the toilets. His enthusiasm for the National Socialist New Order took about three weeks to evaporate, and we never heard of him again.

3. *The informer always wants names and addresses.* He eagerly volunteers to help with mailings of bulletins and newspapers, for in-

stance, because he can get a dekko at the mailing list. He always carries scratch paper or a little notebook so he can get names and phone numbers of new people. He has a great memory for license plates and a great interest in cars. ("Say, what year of Pontiac is that you're drivin', brother?") He is fascinated by guns — he loves to pick them up, handle them, gaze long and closely at the serial numbers, find out all about where people got them, how many other weapons they own, what their firearms experience is like, etc.

4. *The informer likes to wander. You* will find him everywhere, especially around your home or office. You will find him rummaging through drawers on some pretext or other, looking for a match or a pen or whatever. You will find him peeping into your garage, your bedroom, your office or workroom, your darkroom, your printing workshop, wherever he has no business. You will run into him accidentally on purpose on the street. He will always be around, popping up at odd hours, calling you for interminable and pointless conversations.

5. The informer loves to talk about things violent and illegal. This is the mark of the *agent provocateur,* a beastie somewhat different from the straight stool pigeon. Always, he somehow manages to get the conversation around to bombings, shootings, sabotage, anything and everything that your activity unit should not be concerning itself with in Phases One, Two, and Three. You will note he waxes especially insurrectionary on the telephone, which is more than likely tapped and recording your conversations. He has mysterious "contacts" who can get you hand grenades, explosives, machine guns, anti-tank rockets, poison gas, MAC-10 submachine guns, stolen government vehicles, Claymore mines, tactical nuclear warheads, any damned thing that you want except the cash and office supplies you really need to run a legal political group. Funny thing about those "contacts' of his — they can get you virtually anything illegal, no sweat, but ask them to come up with a few rolls of postage stamps or a few hundred bucks as a donation? Not on your nelly!

6. The informer is hard to find. He is very leery of letting you know where he lays his head at night. He is personally security-conscious to the point of paranoia. This is because he usually has a lot to be paranoid about; very often you are not the first group of people, political or merely criminal, that he has squealed on. Informing is a bad habit that is very hard to break once acquired; quite often his "case officer" or "control" down at police headquarters or the Federal building won't let him get out once he's in deep.

7. An informer's cover story often doesn't check out. Insofar as possible, run background checks on anyone you suspect. There are all manner of ways of doing this. We live in a complex society and it is very hard for anyone to hide their real life story from someone else who knows the ropes. Cultivate the art of tracking down and dredging up information about people. It's not only a vital intelligence function and crucial to your safety, it's also fun and a challenge, a mental exercise as good as any board game. I won't go into further detail on this because it's a subject all on its own.

Finally, I must repeat my warning about female agents. Most White racial nationalist activists are still males, for various reasons mostly having to do with the fact that White males are most immediately, personally affected by this society's crapulous sickness and tyranny and therefore have been the first to wake up. Female participation in the Movement is increasing, a development I welcome, but the fact is that we still have too few sisters in the struggle and most of those who are involved are married. This shortage of eligible females is a very serious Achilles heel for us, and the enemy knows this fact and utilizes it.

It is very difficult for a White Aryan male with normal instincts and our people's inbred sense of honor, trust, and decency to entertain the suspicion that his sex partner who has shared the most intimate and personal part of his life may be a deadly enemy. When this happens, it is often more emotionally and spiritually shattering for the man than a JDL bomb or a harassment bust by the FBI would be. Obviously we can't go chasing off any attractive young women who show an interest in our strapping young lads or else we'd lose the strapping young lads in short order. Be alert, be professional in your relationships with women — i.e.,. don't indulge in pillow talk about Movement business — and it wouldn't hurt to check out your people's girl friends. And yours as well.

While on this subject, I want to pass on an imperative piece of advice. *Never, EVER allow yourself to get into a situation where you are alone with a non-White female, a woman police officer, or a woman reporter.* If business compels you to deal with women of this nature, always make sure you're in a group, in a public place, or otherwise chaperoned.

Twice in my experience, White activists have been lured into compromising positions by women who then cried "rape!" In both cases these women were Jewesses who were very White-looking, members of the JDL who went under-cover for this specific purpose. (Perhaps one of them was married to another Jew named Potiphar? I do recall that one of our victims in the L.A. case was named Joseph.) In one case there were arrests in a blaze of very, very bad publicity. They busted our guys in NS uniform during a meeting and the front-page photos showed them being taken into the copshop in handcuffs while the headlines screamed "NAZIS RAPE JEWISH GIRL!" Neither of the cases came to trial because in both instances our people handled it in the only way possible. The local head of the Jewish Defense League was confronted, a pistol produced in order to get his attention, (in one case shoved into his mouth and the hammer cocked), and it was then explained to the filthy kike that there were certain rules in the game of alternative politics and that phony rape accusations were breaking the rules. In both cases the women complainants never showed up in court and our brothers were released, hopefully to exercise more caution in the future, viz., where they stick it.

It may be commented that the preceding anecdote seems to violate my prohibition against illegal activity. Not so. My injunction to all of you *is to survive and carry out your missions.* Right now, breaking the law and going to prison for the remainder of your natural life is counter-survival, and thus to be avoided. Going to prison on a bum rape rap would have the same effect. It, too, is counter-survival. My message in all this is simple: do whatever you have to do to win. That's the ultimate "trick of the trade."

VII.
THE TRICKS OF THE TRADE
(continued)

More handy-dandy hints for the White revolutionary:

The Basic Literature Line. You should maintain an adequate stock of pamphlets, leaflets, and other short items explaining your organization's program and ideas on race, the economy, the Jewish question, the reconstruction of society, and so on. Organize this basic line of short, readable literature into small packets containing six or eight items, and never be without a few in your car or in your home or workplace, so that you can strike while the iron is hot if you feel you've got a good prospect. You should never give people big, thick, heavy books to read until they are already "hooked." Their initial contact with the Movement should be you and your face-to-face conversation, followed by the BLL. The pieces in this basic introductory pack should be short, easy to read, graphically excellent, and with as many pictures and drawings as possible. Bearing in mind the decreasing literacy levels of the entire American population, including the White community, all written material given to prospective recruits should be as simple as possible to begin with. Later on, once they are at least half-way committed and you know they are sufficiently literate and intelligent to read and understand, then you can try them on the big thick books such as *Mein Kampf* or *Which Way Western Man?* or *Imperium.*

I have found that two works by George Lincoln Rockwell, the pamphlet *In Hoc Signo Vinces* and his major work *White Power* are excellent starters for the beginner in racial awareness. They are simply written, incisive and to the point, and not overly long. Another thing you need to start your novices on very early is Holocaust revisionism. Your Basic Literature Line should contain at least one anti-Holocaust leaflet, such as a quick commentary on the Anne Frank fraud. The next step should be Harwood's *Did Six Million Really Die?* Remember, the so-called Holocaust is the Jews' major remaining moral foundation for legitimizing their depredations on society and the atrocities committed by Israel in the Middle East. The world is shocked and angered by what the Jews are doing but keeps stumbling over the extermination lie, the constant screaming and kvetching about the alleged horrors of Auschwitz, etc. Strip that away from them and all you've got are a rat-pack of liars, thieves, and petty gangsters. The world is getting pretty weary of the Jew and his carry-on, and it would take very little to persuade the comity of nations to step on these insects, once the Holocaust hoax is disposed of.

Study the "witnessing" and propaganda distribution techniques of groups such as the Jehovah's Witnesses and the Pentecostalists. The Mormons have the whole missionary drill down to a fine art and their tactics would well repay study. Never be afraid to learn from other movements, right wing or left wing. Bear in mind that whatever avenues or channels of communication you are using with your local White community, the enemy will be seeking to interdict and close off. Have alternate plans available so that when ZOG shuts down one form of informational distribution or agitprop, you can switch over to another channel without any interruption.

Defunctionalization. If you are sufficiently active, then you will eventually be identified by the enemy and targeted for victimization. From their point of view it is essential that you be made an example of in order to frighten other White people away from any involvement in racial nationalist or other dissident politics. In some countries, National Socialists or White racial nationalists are simply hauled away and looked up. In this country, the enemy game plan calls for a bit more subtlety. The most insidious feature of democracy is that it maintains a pretense of freedom for Whites while denying them freedom and self-determination in fact. This keeps them more or less contented, and above all, it keeps them *working,* producing the actual wealth of society and maintaining the System in existence.

The enemy may eventually lock you up as well, either because you have been so stupid as to break the law and give them a handle on you, or else by fabricating evidence that you have committed a crime and paying an informer, with cash or leniency, for his own crimes to get up on a witness stand and swear your life away. However, their first and primary weapon against White political dissent is defunctionalization, the blacklisting of known White racists in a locality and a refusal to allow them to earn a living and thus survive in so-called "legitimate" society.

Defunctionalization is no longer quite so effective as it was, because in many areas of the United States there is a shortage of peon-type labor and a really determined White can always fall back on turning burgers, pushing broom, or the night shift at the Quik-Pik. This isn't much help if you've been making $12.00 an hour as a skilled mechanic or $16.00 an hour as a plumber or whatever and you have to drop down to minimum wage at the Burger King. However, burger-doodling is at least a job. In 1977 I was blacklisted in Raleigh by the ADL and the boycott was so total that between then and 1981 when I left town I worked a total of three days on paper, legally. Nor was it for lack of my trying. I put in around 200 applications over the years 1977 and 1978 and in a couple of cases I was almost hired until my routine pre-employment credit check came back with "contact Goldstein's Fashion Outlets for special ref." (The Jew who ran this chain of shops was the local ADL district chairman.) After that it wasn't necessary to defunctionalize me, because I was in the papers all the time and in any case I had given up trying.

Today, I don't *think* it would be possible for the ADL to do this because Raleigh has become so Yuppiefied that the labor shortage has reached acute proportions and Raleigh businesses are starting to import Chinese and Sikhs to turn their burgers and man their cash registers. My guess is that when I get targeted again and lose my present job I'll be able to burger-doodle or do something at minimum wage because businesses are so crucially short of competent (i.e. White) help.

This doesn't apply in all areas, of course. Also, I am single (now) and mobile and I can afford to up stakes and go where the work is. For the married man with a family, a mortgage, and roots in the community the threat of defunctionalization is deadly. There is virtually no legal recourse available. I have yet to hear of any White nationalist anywhere successfully contesting a politically-motivated dismissal in court or getting any kind of compensation at all, never mind being re-hired. Defunctionalization is actually a worse threat to us than being framed for spurious "crimes." It is most effective, since a man fighting for economic survival is hardly in any case to engage in unauthorized political activity. It is cost-effective from their point of view and doesn't expose them to the same risk that fabricating criminal charges can do; bogus "evidence" and perjured testimony has a nasty habit of coming unglued, sometimes years afterwards, and these incidents can be embarrassing to Yuppies in three-piece suits.

There are several ways in which the System conveys its wishes to your boss in the matter of your continued employment. First, the media have a bash at it. Once you are identified, your name, address, and place of employment are splattered all over the front page of the local newspaper, generally along with a photograph of you which has been arranged or in some eases doctored to make you look as ugly and foolish and undesirable as possible. Often this alone is enough to do the trick: you come in to work the next morning and a pink slip awaits. The media may also try phoning you at work, coming around to "interview" you at work, hanging around in the parking lot harassing your co-workers with inane questions. ("Did you know Bill Jones was a neo-Nazi/Klansman/right-wing radical? Did you know he carries a gun? Did you know members of his organization were arrested by the FBI for conspiracy to blow up elementary schools full of little children?") Very few businesses can take this kind of treatment for long.

If that doesn't do it, the next step is generally a visit from your friendly neighborhood FBI. Needless to say, they just *couldn't* fit it into their busy schedules to ask you their "routine questions" at home or over the weekend and they just *had* to come and see you at work with their drivel. A favorite trick is to interview you in the presence of your supervisor or boss, "just so he'll know everything is on the up-and-up." Their questions then deal with guns, bombs, your associations with real or alleged criminal elements, your acquaintance with other racial nationalists who have been convicted rightfully or wrongfully of violent illegal acts, etc. They will also mention the admittedly real possibility that you and your workplace may be the victim of gun or arson attacks by the Left or the JDL. By the time they leave, your boss has a case of the screaming meemies and your days as an employee there are numbered.

Failing that, there is always extra-legal pressure from the ADL or the violent, radical Left. It will be made clear to your employer that as long as he keeps you on he will not get certain contracts and customers as heretofore, or he will sometimes be offered an especially big customer or a plum contract if he fires you. He may find himself suddenly unable to obtain supplies of a crucial raw material or item that the business must have in order to function. His regular customers will suddenly turn elsewhere for their orders. He will suddenly find himself the subject of sales tax audits and IRS investigations. He will find his credit with suppliers cut off and cash on the barrel head demanded for every purchase, a basis upon which very few businesses nowadays can operate. Every day he will get the message that one of his employees is definitely not kosher. This sort of subtle pressure is what the Jews excel at, the technique they have developed and refined for thousands of years, ever since Joseph cornered the Egyptian grain market and Yehudi found that taking a "cut" of the gentile's labor was so much more easy and profitable than working. Money is a tool, but it can also be an instrument that the Jew plays like a virtuoso when he's of a mind to. It is the one thing they're really good at.

Unless your boss is a man (or woman) of really exceptional character, he will not be able to withstand this symphony of shekels for long. There are, however, still other arrows in the enemy's quiver to shoot at your paycheck. When the ultra-Left or the JDL gets in on the act, things can get very hairy. They may picket your workplace, with resultant unfavorable media attention. They may stone or slash the tires of your company's delivery vehicles. They may break the windows in the plant or the office. They may attack you outside your job or burn your car in the parking lot. They may firebomb your shop or showroom in the dead of night, or fire shots from speeding cars. All of these things have happened to me or to people I have known, and together they form a pattern of intimidation and harassment that is almost impossible for any employer to withstand.

Another set of problems you may have at the workplace will come not from outsiders, but from the affirmative action niggers and spics, and in some cases Reds if you're in a large factory or installation. If you work in a unionized plant they may threaten to go on strike if you are not dismissed. (This is how I was booted from Hillhaven Convalescent Home in Raleigh, in August of 1977. The black nursing and kitchen staff threatened to walk out and I was fired within the hour.) If there is any Communist infiltration on your shop floor you may be attacked in dark corners, your car's tires will be slashed or your gas tank sugared, etc. (One quick little trade secret: always have a lock on your gas cap and if possible on your hood as well. They love to trash your car.)

Countering Defunctionalization. First off, bear in mind that, as always, the pressure you are subjected to on the job will be in direct proportion to the level of overt activity you are engaged in. A lot of people reading this will say, "Hell, everybody where I work knows how I feel about niggers and Jews and I've never had any such trouble as you describe!" Maybe not, but I'll bet those who make this claim haven't been active beyond a certain level, either. Attempted or actual defunctionalization is, in a way, a back-handed sort of a compliment, They don't come after you unless you've gotten them rattled.

If your boss is non-White or Jewish, then you've got problems and you probably won't last too long once you get identified and targeted. If he is White, though, try to cultivate a good relationship with him. Make him like and respect you as a person. *Carefully* sound him out on his own political and racial views. If and when the time seems ripe, let him know that you're at least peripherally involved with such-and-such a group, Don't let the media catch him by surprise when they call his home at ten o'clock at night and ask him, "Did you know your foreman Jim Johnson is a violent racist extremist?" If you've adequately prepped and warned him, he can say something other than "duuuuuhhuh?" If you haven't given him any warning, then when the excrement hits the revolving blades he may feel that you have betrayed him and left him hanging out to dry, vulnerable and turning slowly in the wind. I should mention, though, that if your boss shows any signs of left-wing or liberal views or just plain swinish stupidity (not an uncommon characteristic among our Peter Principle managerial class), then you should leave him be. Don't look for trouble before it starts.

When you do get fired, don't let it catch you flat-footed. You should have known it would come eventually and you should be prepared for it. If at all possible, try to have a financial reserve to fall back on, a savings account stashed somewhere containing at least three months' net salary, more if possible. I know that's hard to do in these times, and it's almost impossible to do when you're politically active and the Movement is guzzling your disposable income like a bottomless pit. Try to get that done during Phase One, the initial recruitment and preparation phase.

Always keep an eye out for job opportunities and sources of extra income. Even if you don't have time now, file them away for future reference. A mail order business or consulting business is best, because it means that *you are not dependent upon your immediate geographical locality for your income.* This makes it very difficult for the enemy to locate and choke off all your sources of income, although they can bring pressure on media you advertise with not to carry your ads, try and get you arrested for "mail fraud" if your paperwork isn't 100% squared away, harass you with local ordinances, etc. A cottage industry of some kind is also very good, making and selling little knicknacks to tourists or flogging them by mail. If you have access to some agricultural land, even a fairly large garden, you can grow vegetables and fruit for sale at farmers' markets and flea markets. You can become a used goods dealer, buying and selling anything and everything in flea markets or door to door. (Don't knock it, it's how most Jews got their start.)

Needless to say, the places of employment and sources of income of White racial nationalists are a primary item that the enemy seeks to ascertain. All information pertaining to the economic status of you *and* your White comrades is to be treated with the highest security precautions and anyone who seems inordinately interested in finding out where everyone works is to be regarded with suspicion.

White Co-ops. One of the ideas I have always wanted to try is that of forming White economic co-operatives to help sustain our people, help their families make it economically in these hard times, and above all, to cushion our people against the devastating effects of defunctionalization and Judaic economic assault. The idea is that everyone in a group bands together and agrees to provide certain goods and services to the other members of the group free of charge. One or two provide auto repairs and routine maintenance for only the cost of the parts. Farmers and gardeners provide fruits and vegetables. Shop owners and retailers provide goods at wholesale cost. Members kick into pools of money to buy large case lots of canned goods, detergents, household goods, toilet paper, whatever and the resultant mass purchase is distributed equally among the participants. Members kick in to buy communal items of hardware, appliances, lawn mowers, tools, etc, which are then shared. A communal library of books and other material is created for research, education, and propaganda purposes. The possibilities are endless.

The establishment of White economic co-operatives should be a major point of urgency with the Movement. There are already some rudimentary co-ops and similar ventures in operation, mostly on the West Coast and mostly run by Identity and other groups on the religious right. It is an idea that needs to be adopted far more widely than it is. The next major steps along this line will involve not only providing goods and services for our own people but *jobs* for our own people, and then after that, providing goods and services and finally jobs for Whites within the community in general.

If a White co-operative movement can ever get going, we can undermine the most deadly stranglehold of the enemy: *the necessity of selling our skills and our labor to the System in order to survive!* Subverting that iron-handed method of controlling White dissent will be a victory of earth-shaking proportions.

ENEMY VIOLENCE

If you are in any way politically active and you stick with it, eventually you are going to be physically assaulted by the enemy. The object of these attacks is not so much to hurt you as an individual but, once again, to *make an example* of you in order to frighten off other Whites and prevent them from supporting you. In this, it is generally a successful tactic, I'm afraid, largely due to media misrepresentations of these incidents.

In actual fact, our people generally do pretty well against physical attackers. It should be borne in mind that many attacks consist of a single blow or whack with a weapon and are staged strictly for the media in order to get the White racist's picture in the papers receiving a blow, never giving one in return. The attackers either whack you or sock you while the cameras click and then run away rapidly, or else they are immediately grabbed by conveniently hovering police before you can wade into them and hustled off to the station house where they will pay a $10 forfeiture fine and return to a standing ovation in the synagogue or the feminist consciousness-raising class.

However, in a genuine knock-down drag-out fight we've done some real damage, especially when we've been able to corner the cowardly and despicable Jewish Defense League. JDL hebes have gone to the hospital with all manner of broken heads and broken bones, and generally after one good punch-up they learn which of our activity units to leave alone. Significantly, they have yet to bother us down here in North Carolina. Us Southern boys with the Confederate flag bumper stickers and rifle racks in our pick-up trucks are a mite too formidable opponents for the pimple-faced yeshiva boys from Brooklyn. They prefer eighty-year-old Eastern Europeans with white canes and hearing aids as fitting targets for their vaunted *barzel.*

The only time any of our people have ever been seriously hurt, either by JDL or by Communists, is when we have been outnumbered by absolutely staggering odds. In my first major JDL confrontation, in Lafayette Park, eight National Socialists stood off a good fifty kikes with clubs and busted a couple of their hook noses pretty good. It is largely because of the pusillanimous showing that the Jewish Defense League's "troops" have made in physical confrontations with our people and with assorted Arabs and Russians that the JDL has switched to bombing, vandalism, and arson. In this manner they have actually inflicted some very serious damage on Arabs and Soviets and elderly Eastern Europeans, including the contemptible, revoltingly cruel mutilation and murder of Tscherim Soobzokov.

Many enemy assaults will take place in connection with White racial nationalist media appearances. In the old days, they sometimes staged attacks at public demonstrations, turning them into "rock festivals" where a small handful of our people were pelted with flying objects by Jews or the rent-a-mob Reds. You shouldn't be engaging in this type of pointless activity, so I won't go into that. However, sometimes media appearances may be deemed necessary and you will be attacked inside or outside of the television studio, the press conference, whatever. The key element here is that your presence will in some manner have been *announced in advance,* so the enemy knows that you will be at a certain place at a certain time.

Another place where you have to be on your guard is courtrooms, when you are dealing with some hearing or Mickey Mouse rap and again they know when and where you will be. A tip: often media people, even when asked to keep your appearance on a talk show or interview secret, will deliberately *call the Reds or JDL* and tip them off that you are coming, either in order to stage a confrontation for their cameras or else for purely ideological reasons, hoping that you will be injured or killed. I cannot emphasize too strongly that media personnel are enemies and must be treated as such. Their word is not worthy of trust and their version of such "regrettable occurrences" does not merit belief.

Whenever you are going into a situation of this kind, take as many friends and comrades as you can with you, not only as fighters but as witnesses. If you find you can't get anyone to go with you, then these people are chickenshit and you need to get a new set of friends and comrades. Deliberately exposing yourself to identification and retaliation through stupid public "rallies" is one thing: letting a brother walk into an enemy ambush alone is another. If you can't get your people to risk a few punches, you're not going to be able to get them to risk anything greater. Can them and start over. In this the JDL and Communists perform a valuable function in helping us weed out the Nervous Nellies and the poltroonish hobbyists. (I need hardly add that no stigma need be attached to a comrade or supporter of seventy-five who declines to go on such escort duty, nor should you take elderly or female comrades on such runs.)

Anytime you believe there to be any risk of an enemy attack at any kind of function your duty requires you to attend, *watch your car.* They love to slash tires and smash windshields. Leave a guard on your car, or better yet, take two cars in case one gets hit. If possible, take enough men to throw out scouting parties, along with walkie-talkies for communications. If you have an HQ or office with a CB base station, keep in contact with your own 'CB. Whenever you can, scout the area in advance. Note the entrances and exits to the studio or auditorium, the layout of the building. Familiarize yourself with what security precautions your hosts may provide. Tell them flat out beforehand that there may be trouble and you're not going to run from it if there is; the thought of a hundred thousand dollars worth of damage to their high-tech studio equipment or lawsuits from bystanders who get hurt may concentrate their minds wonderfully.

Put yourself in the enemy commander's position. How would you attack your group or a similar one if the situation was reversed? Where would you park your own transport? How would you enter the building? How would you get past the plant security or the alarms? What kind of weapons would you bring and what kind of propaganda effect would you aim for? This is good practice, brothers, because one day the situation *will* be reversed and we will be giving this garbage a taste of their own medicine.

The Attack. It is my experience that an actual assault almost never comes completely without warning. They may call you on the telephone and gibber threats at you days beforehand if they know where you are going to be that far in advance. You will probably be able to spot them milling around wherever it is when you pull up in the parking lot or nearby street. A standard tactic of most enemy factions seems to be to show up at the TV studio or wherever about half an hour early. You can possibly thwart an attack as you go in by pitching up an hour early yourself, gaining admittance, and sitting around with your party in a waiting room or cafeteria shooting the breeze. Then you only have to worry about coming out.

If you are going on a talk show, you should be alert and prepared to defend yourself even while you are sitting, ostensibly at ease, talking to the host or the panel or whatever. Some groups will infiltrate the studio audience, and then storm the stage on a pre-arranged signal. Your escorts should always be in the wings, ready to leap forward and wade in.

On concluding your business, you should leave the building by a pre-arranged route so that you can rendezvous with your transport as quickly as possible and leave the area. *Never, ever hang around in the immediate vicinity once you have done taping or speechifying or whatever you're doing there,*

When the enemy sights you, the attack will generally begin with a lot of screaming, name-calling, and gabbling filthy words, rather like primitive tribes in New Guinea making ritual rushes with their spears or a gorilla beating his chest. (The similarities are sometimes more than coincidental.) You will note that our racial enemies generally display a distinct lack of imagination, referring to you by one of three obscene words, the "f" word, the "mf" one, and the "s" word, in some combination with the word "bastard". (As an etomological aside, note the contrast between the paucity of the Jews' and Reds' maledictory vocabulary compared with our own rich nomenclature for them. I have counted a dozen derogatory terms we Whites use for "communist", at least two dozen for "Jew," and over a hundred for "nigger." But I digress.)

Verbal abuse will generally be followed by the throwing of objects if you're in the open and they have room to do so, including rocks, bottles, brick, eggs, rotten fruit, balloons full of urine, bags of faeces, etc. (The Jewish obsession with excretion and body waste comes into full play here.) Sometimes that's all it takes in order to accomplish their objectives. If there are police present, they can move in, declare the event a "riot" and turn back or arrest the Whites while allowing the Reds or Jews to scamper off unmolested. The enemy can then claim a "victory" wherein the "outrage of the people stopped the fascists from speaking" or whatever. (They will do so in any case. Reds are never defeated in the pages of their own rags, or if they are overwhelmingly beaten their casualties become "glorious martyrs." Not a bad propaganda technique actually, and one which we could well emulate.)

If you are actually attacked, don't lose your cool. You should have prepared for the eventuality and organized your reaction with your escort. Part of your training, which should be ongoing throughout the first three organizational phases, should be the art and science of defending yourself and inflicting as much damage as you possibly can with your bare hands. You should know how to parry blows with weapons so that the weapons are deflected and don't whiplash your arm or face, how to parry knives and broken bottles, etc. *Never, ever carry weapons* to any possible confrontation or you will be arrested and the System will have its handle on you for a long, long time. The one occasional exception to this is Mace or something similar, *where such substances are legal under state law to begin with,* and even then it can be dicey. When attacked, you will always be outnumbered by a very large ratio. Indeed, I have never known any attack against any of our people on anything remotely resembling equal odds. I have been in alternative politics of some kind now for almost twenty years, and I can truthfully say that *never,* not once in all that time, have I ever heard of a Jew or a Communist or even yahoo White assholes offering to fight any Klan or National Socialist group on a one-to-one basis. This says something about us and it says something about the kind of people who oppose us.

If they get you down, don't try to get up at first because that exposes you; they're waiting for it and will hit you in the gut, the groin, and the head with the boot. If you stay down, they'll either back off or more likely try the boot anyway. Curl up, protect your head and groin, but keep your eyes open as best you can. When one of them gets too close in order to kick you, grab his ankle, using both hands, and *twist hard!* This will break or dislocate his ankle, and more importantly, *bring him down* so that you can pull him close to you and use him as a shield. If there is a wall anywhere near at all, roll over to it and hold onto that hebe or commie, using him as a shield against the others' boots. A good hold is one hand on his throat, another on his crotch, and your teeth sunk into something fleshy on his face for good measure. He may well be doing the same to you, but you're White and so you take the pain and keep hold of him. Walk yourself up, your back against the wall, then fling him hard into the milling enemy either to the right or left while you bounce and clobber another one in the opposite direction.

Now, there is one thing that you must decide on as a matter of firm policy before you enter into any possibly confrontational situation. If an enemy attacks you, physically assaults you in an effort to deny you your rights under the United States Constitution, then he is in the wrong despite the fact that you will probably take the fall. You must determine, absolutely, that this is something you will not tolerate and you must let the enemy know that in no uncertain terms, by speaking to him in the only language that he understands, brute force. If he is a Communist, then he already worships naked force as an ideology in any case. If he is a Jew, then he instinctively knows from thousands of years of racial memory when the *goy* is aroused. Winston Churchill said that the Jew is always either at your throat or at your feet, and he knows when to change tack.

If, during an enemy-initiated confrontation, you get hold of a Jew or a Communist, *hurt him. Hurt him badly.* Make him bleed. Break his bones. Make his face look like something one orders in a Mexican restaurant. Carefully study and train yourself in the art of making a mess of the human body. Rupture his eardrums. Knock out his teeth. Squash his nose into a rubbery mass. Put him on crutches if you can, or better yet, in a wheelchair. Don't kill him if you can help it. You don't want to give the enemy a martyr, you want to give them a living, bleeding example of what will happen to people who try to forcibly deny White Americans their rights in their own land that their forefathers fought and worked for.

You will probably get in some degree of trouble over this, depending on the circumstances, but something absolutely vital is at stake here and it is worth the risk. These left-wing and Zionist terrorist groups are an important part of the enemy's strategy. They are the stick just as the color TVs and the RVs and the video games are the carrot. Their purpose is to suppress White dissent by force if all else fails, which is why the state allows them to exist and in some cases to flourish, arresting them only when they get completely out of hand. Meeting and defeating this type of hooliganism is one of the many tests and obstacles that the White revolutionary party is going to have to face and overcome. It is an unavoidable part of the progress of our movement. It is best faced up to and gotten over with early on before we have to take on the really major enemy formations.

I am not coming on with this 1930s "battle for the streets" rhetoric we occasionally hear from the Hollywood Nazis and such. The streets don't belong to us or to the Reds, they belong to the System. But we cannot function if we have to constantly fool around with these JDL and lefty idiots. Under no circumstances whatsoever must we allow them to delay or deflect our advancement. We must teach them unequivocally that if they attempt to interfere with us they will be hurt and that in this case we are not afraid to do what has to be done in spite of their Big Brother protectors. Very few of these jerks actually believe in Marxism or Kahane or whatever enough to undergo certain pain and injury.

A final hint on the gang attack: when going into a confrontational situation, always wear a codpiece or athletic protector. Our enemies are very prone towards low blows.

To Pack or Not to Pack? At some stage you are going to have to decide upon a policy, either personally or within your activity unit, as to when and where and under what circumstances you and your comrades will carry a gun. This is a very grey area and I can really offer no cut-and-dried advice.

On the one hand, I have been saved from violent assault on several occasions by the presence of a firearm on my person. I know quite well that one of the reasons none of our North Carolina functions on private property were ever attacked was the presence of weapons and our known willingness to use them. On the other hand, excessive display of weaponry gets ZOG very, very nervous and in my view tends to bring down unnecessary and premature heat. I also recall one occasion when I had to restrain one of my men from shooting dead a burr-headed nigger in the parking lot of a convenience store, something that would have gotten about fourteen people, including myself, jugged for some kind of "conspiracy." On one hand, weapons are necessary for home defense in the ordinary course of daily life here in these Jewnited States, given the presence of niggers in our society and the refusal of the régime to control or discipline them in any way. On the other hand, the cops can pull you over on a dark night, blast you, stick your car gun into your dead hand, and then claim, "Gee, I pulled him over for a traffic violation and he pulled a gun on me!"

My general advice would be: carry a gun in any situation where there may be an actual threat to life and limb. Otherwise don't risk it. It's a fine line indeed and there is room for debate and wide latitude for flexibility here. Be careful, though. Once the bullet leaves the barrel of a gun it can never be taken back. Once you have shot someone, even in self defense, you are in a whole new world of danger and hassles beyond belief. A gun is like fire — it can save your life, or it can destroy it. Carlyle wrote that gunpowder makes all men tall; it imparts a deceptive feeling of power. I like guns, for the same reasons that I recognize their dangerously seductive addiction. God made man, but Colonel Colt made him equal. It's a good feeling to know that .44 in your hand makes you able to take out the biggest nigger in the Chicago offensive line, makes people listen to what you have to say, makes people fear you. Don't let it carry you away.

Guns are a tool in this revolution, no more, no less. We will acquire them when we need to use them and use them as the situation demands, but I see no point whatsoever in loading up with all manner of weaponry and ammunition that will never be fired at the enemy. Nor is there any need to break the law and acquire machine guns and grenades and rocket launchers and all this mess. I have served in the military and I can tell you that, unless you are properly trained in the use of automatic weapons, a machine gun is more dangerous to you than it is to anyone you may tangle with. For home defense all you need is a twelve-gauge shotgun; in any underground situation with ten minutes and a hacksaw you can shorten the barrel, take off the stock and *voila!* you have the most deadly personal close-quarters weapon ever invented.

If I myself were going to go underground and play urban guerrilla, I wouldn't fool with these little machine pistols that burp a thirty-round magazine in five seconds and gobble ammunition like popcorn. I'd get myself one good, long-range sniper's rifle with a scope; one compact, concealable yet heavy handgun like a .44 Bulldog, .357 snub or a .380 automatic; some disposable small-caliber Saturday Night Specials for one-shot assassination work and then discard; and for my weapon of choice to tickle Yehudi's liver I'd pack a sawed-off twelve. With rare exceptions I wouldn't fire double-ought buckshot; in a sawed-off gun that heavy charge will cause the weapon to kick like a Missouri mule and throw your pattern way off. Number four shot is the ticket at the ranges we're speaking of.

I might add that all the foregoing advice is available legally in various System publications and all of the weapons I have mentioned are also legal, so long as the shotgun is (at time of this writing) 18 inches or more in the barrel and 26 inches or more overall. However, I have no intention of spending my money any time soon on any of these guns, I don't need guns right now and neither do you. We need postage stamps, printing, graphic and layout equipment, telephones, desks, transportation, literature, office space, filing cabinets, posters and stickers, tabloid newspapers and smaller newsletters, filing fees for political office candidacies, and such. Guns are just expensive toys right now, in any quantity greater than one or two: necessary to defend your home and to carry in your car.

The Cup That Cheers. A brief word about alcohol. It is here It is with us. It is a part of our heritage from the days of Xenophon to the beer halls of Munich. Yes, it is a drug. No, it is *not* a drug in the same sense that marijuana and cocaine are drugs. There is absolutely no point in trying to prohibit its use, or forbid it to our people completely. That was tried in Prohibition and it failed.

Alcohol and politics, however, do not mix. Furthermore, alcoholics fall into the same category as Jews and homosexuals as far as potential membership goes. Avoid drunks like the plague. Do not admit them into membership and do not allow them to worm their way into any party function. They tend to corrupt moderate drinkers and disrupt events. A free and pleasant social life between White comrades is vital, creating a sense of community and a closeness that we must have. Each organization and activity unit must figure out its own way to deal with and regulate alcohol in the social aspects of its function, but alcohol should *never* be present during any actual business meeting or political function. Nor should any political discussion or attempt at recruitment *ever* take place in a bar or in any kind of alcoholic setting. I might add that the above *rule* does not apply in Europe, where the pub and the beer garden perform an entirely different social function than the roadhouse or bar in America. Indeed, the two are almost totally dissimilar, just as European and American society are almost totally dissimilar.

DEALING WITH THE MEDIA

The best idea is to avoid the media as long as you can. They are going to slander you, distort your views, incite your enemies to attack you, and do their best to discredit you, because that is their function in the scheme of things, but there is no reason why you should help them attain these goals. The major strategy should always be to build our own networks of communications directly between us and the White community, bypassing their cameras and newspapers altogether where possible. We must present our message directly to our own people without allowing them to filter it and distort it through their editing, their tricks, and their lies.

However, in a practical sense it will be impossible to avoid the media completely. Sometimes it may be necessary to give them something to chew on in order to distract their attention from something that the group is doing which they don't need to pry into. Sometimes it may be necessary in order to counter enemy disinformation as best we can or to spread disinformation of our own. Sometimes we may be running an election campaign or a strike or some other project wherein it is necessary to use every possible method to get our message to the White voter or citizen. Other times we may need to use the media for widescale distribution of an idea or a concept and then use the White reaction as a gauge and a sounding board. Finally, and most importantly, the media can use our persistent non-coöperation against us. I was once "invited" to a candidates' forum in one of my election campaigns, only the television station conveniently mislaid my invitation. The whole program was then turned into an attack on the "horrors of racism" with all the other candidates bleating in chorus, "Black skin good, white skin baaaaaad!" The camera focused on an empty chair with my name on it.

During Phase One, the enemy, ZOG and media both, should have no idea at all that there is any racialist activity in their area, at least not insofar as your WRP is concerned, although others may be stirring it. During Phase Two, you will probably start getting requests at your post office box or public address for interviews. If you have a telephone number listed they will call you, but bear in mind that they have contacts in the phone company they use for such purposes and they will find out your address that way, whereupon they will rock up on your doorstep at eight in the morning when you leave for work, follow you to your job, etc. It is always a mistake to let the media know where you live, if you can prevent them from finding out. Your house will be pictured on TV and in the newspapers, your neighbors and your family will he harassed, and the whole thing is a deliberate implicit invitation to enemy paramilitaries and thugs to attack your home.

COMPREHENSION. Media people are completely devoid of any sense of morality, decency, embarrassment, or shame. Of all our enemies other than the Jews themselves, media people are the most morally bankrupt.

You may recall the infamous incident wherein a liberated lady newshen from one of the major networks was interviewing a woman whose three children had just died in a fire, which was still smouldering in the background. "I know how you feel," clucked the wretched TV bitch. "I had a kitten that died once,"

Reporters and television personalities are on the biggest ego trip going in today's society. Their power is in many cases greater than that of the government because they are believed and the government is not, and they know this. They live for the sight of their own face on that tube and their own voice on the sound speakers; having grown up in the boob-tubular society, they are convinced that television is the true reality and since they're on TV every day, they're more real than the rest of us. All the earth is one big news story to them and all the rest of humanity are extras and stage props for their "art." They are the priests and hierophants of the Almighty Tube. Bow down, peasants, before the Great God Television's Anointed!

Newspaper and magazine reporters are almost as big a group of assholes. They all think they're Woodward and Bernstein or else Ernest Hemingway with a word processor. There are a *few* good reporters working for the smaller papers, but the minute they print an objective article about anything White and racial nationalist they find themselves on the obituary desk or on the street. Reporters have a very keen sense viz., which side of their bread is buttered, and if they are uncertain as to the slant an article is supposed to take, their city editor lets them know very quickly. I know — I used to be a reporter myself, once upon a time.

Newspapers, television stations, magazines, and radio stations have no sense of responsibility whatsoever to their readers. Their responsibility is to their owners, and if you look far enough back and deep enough you will find that the controlling interest of every major medium of communications in this country is either Jewish or a person or persons so totally and slavishly devoted to Jewish interests that there is no significant difference. This is not accidental. The Chosen have worked long and hard to bring about precisely the state of affairs that prevails today in the media and no one else gets a look in. No one. They can afford to lose almost every other aspect of their power other than media control. When that goes, they're dead and they know it.

Yet even that is slipping away from them. The trouble with pulling strings from behind the scenes is that the strings sometimes get so thin and tenuous that they break. Some of these "investigative reporters" have gotten so full of themselves that they actually think their job is to *investigate* things! I recently saw a two-hour piece on organized crime done by a big, big name indeed among our media megastars. The advance advertising said that, among other things, the flood of Israeli hoodlums entering this country fleeing from the Arab knives was to be discussed. Not word one on the broadcast. Obviously the Chosen who ran the network were able to pull that section, this time. But what about next time one of their journalistic pets gets stroppy and pokes his nose into something he shouldn't? Or the time after that?

Criticism of Israel is starting to slip past the kosher censors in both the printed and electronic media. Adverse commentary about the Jewish political lobby in Washington; genuinely satirical cartoons about Zionist butchery; genuine reportage of the situation in the West Bank and in the Zionist concentration camps for Palestinians; rude comments about the Zionist spy network in America; critical discussion of the vile practice of handing elderly East Europeans over to the Jews and the Soviet Communists to be murdered; all these have appeared in the media recently. It doesn't indicate that the media are swinging around to our point of view, by any means. It simply means that their egos have gotten so big they are biting the hands that feed them. A little judicious application of Arab money hasn't hurt either. Yehudi is finding out that others can play his game too, and he is really getting uptight.

The first thing you must remember in dealing with any kind of reporter, printed or electronic, is that you are dealing with an egotist. The second thing you must remember is that he or she *is not our friend* however friendly they may come on to you in order to draw you out. Some of the friendliest reporters I've talked to have printed the vilest lies and garbage about me and about the party. The third thing you must remember is that *there is no such thing as "off the record" with any reporter.* When they tell you so, in order to encourage you to talk, they are lying to you. Without exception.

The only way to handle any reporter of any kind, if you absolutely must talk with him or cooperate with him to any degree, is to *maintain 100% control over all the information and impressions that he or she receives.* You control the words they hear, you control the sights they see, you control the people they meet, you control the environment in which the interview takes place, you control the visual images they pick up on their cameras and in their minds. If you are badgered for a print interview, the best way of all is to do it by post, having the paper submit written questions and you providing written answers, making sure of course that those answers are articulate and all correctly spelled. I would, in fact, say that in Phase Two that is the *only* way the WRP should give interviews, although this might not be completely practical.

Pre-recorded television interviews should always be done on your ground, not theirs. If they don't want to do it your way, then they don't do it, end of story. We don't really need them in any case, or rather if we *do* need them, then the WRP is structured wrongly and headed in the wrong direction. If you have any kind of open office or headquarters, one room should be set aside especially for television interviews. This should preferably be an office or library type room, and your background should be book-lined shelves, possibly with a colorful flag or a bust of some imposing great man. Failing that, the interview should be done outdoors, with you or whoever is being interviewed sitting easily but with correct posture, and green leaves of some sort as the backdrop. Never let them interview you standing up. Never let them interview you with an open street, moving traffic, or a blank wall in the background.

Never talk to them while going to a car or into a building; they doctor it to make it look like you're running away from them.,.

Always wear a suit and tie for any interview at all. Get a haircut and make sure your grooming is immaculate. Never, ever let them interview you in your own home. They will find something nasty and disparaging to say about it, making you or your wife out to be slobs, or obsessively neat neurotics if you tidy up for them. Besides, you shouldn't let them know where you live. Try to avoid extemporaneous, unscheduled interviews unless there is something happening that demands your immediate comment. Always choose your words carefully when you do extemporize: remember, with any reporter you are speaking for the permanent record.

If you can't set up the whole interview yourself, the next best thing is to go to the newspaper or television station. Never meet them in, say, a Burger King. Never meet them in a bar or with "Joe sent me" type secrecy. They will use that to make you look ridiculous. Never allow a television camera or any kind of reporter into a unit meeting. Our internal business is our business, not theirs. When you are being filmed or interviewed, don't pick your nose or scratch your behind or betray any type of eccentric or unusual mannerism. They will record it, on film if they can, and make you out to be a spastic looney. Modulate your voice during the interview, remain cool and never allow yourself to get emotional or your voice to become shrill. Treat the reporter with courtesy but keep your distance and never let him get informal or friendly. Remember my previous injunction against being alone with a woman reporter; the one time I think someone might have been trying to set me up for a rape rap the bait they used was an extremely attractive newshen who later turned out to be as Red as a London double-decker bus.

By all means, psych them out if you can but be careful. They're not stupid. Once at the Raleigh headquarters, this kid who came around to help with things dropped a huge bottle of some chemical, iodine I think it was, on the front sidewalk. He then picked up the paper bag containing the broken bottle and carried it around back to the trash, dripping all the way. Whatever this stuff was, it looked for all the world like blood.

A television crew was due any minute, with an especially obnoxious female interviewer. I had a hot flash and told one of the *guys* to go up and get a couple of axe handles we kept upstairs. When the newshen and her crew arrived, they stepped over a big splattered puddle of red-dish-brown liquid. They halted and the fem, sensing a story, followed the "blood trail" around back, where she found it leading over the wall and into the street. (I'd had the kid take the dripping bottle down a block or two and throw it in a dumpster.) She also saw me and two other guys cleaning axe handles of red liquid into a garbage can with newspapers and Brillo and a bucket of water. "Ah, Miss X.," I said. "Come around and I'll let you in the front."

"What if he comes back with the cops?" asked my man, on cue.

"Hell, the son of a bitch deserved it," I said, shrugging. "Call me, but I doubt he'll go to the law." We went inside. The newsfem was all agog and I spun her a tale of negroidal presumption and Southern justice swift and sure, all very casually as if it were the most minor of everyday occurrences. She was nervous throughout the interview and I noted that night that her two-minute clip was remarkably restrained. For some reason, she never came back to sneer at us pathetic Nazi losers, as she once called us. That broken bottle of iodine and my merry little jest had suddenly given her a vision of a future she grooved not upon.

There is nothing like violence or the implicit threat of violence to silence the arrogance and snide ridicule of our enemies. It never hurts to give them occasional little reminders, media people especially, that even though they may treat us like dogs, dogs have teeth. If your unit can inflict some bloodletting on the enemy and get away with it, make sure the media know about it. You will find they treat you with infinitely more respect.

VIII.
WHAT TO DO IF YOU ARE CAPTURED

When every other method of harassment and victimization that the enemy deploys against you fails, they will bring in their ultimate deterrent, the System's ponderous legal and judicial machinery. They will do whatever it takes in order to remove you from circulation and repress the threat that your ideas and your dissenting political activities present to the establishment. You must accept from the very beginning that eventually you will face an attempt to frame you for crimes that you have not committed and falsely to imprison you under color of law. If you are not prepared to accept this, then you should not engage in White racial nationalist activity at all. Be honest with yourself and with your comrades, If you can't stand the heat, stay out of the kitchen.

That's the bad news. The good news is that at the present time of writing it is still possible to beat these attempts. It takes adequate preparation, it takes knowledge of the law's serpentine twists and turns, it takes iron will and steely courage, and it takes a bodacious amount of sheer luck. But it can be done.

This is because the System is not yet ready to throw out the rule book completely and won't be for a long time. You're playing against a heavily stacked deck, but at least you're in the game. Sometimes even the most massive efforts that the System can bring to bear in order to destroy our people still fail. The prime example of this is the ordeal of the Greensboro men, who suffered through the longest criminal trial in the history of the state of North Carolina, a grand-jury witch hunt lasting more than a year, a completely unconstitutional and illegal Federal trial for "civil rights violations," and a harassing private lawsuit from the Communists that lasted for years. Every one of these men came out mentally scarred and spiritually shattered, but some stuck with the Movement despite everything. The only one who ever served a prison sentence as such for Greensboro was one pathetic young man who agreed to cop a plea to the Federals, a living example of the "don't make deals" rule I will be discussing in a bit.

Fabricating the evidence. We will presume for the sake of discussion in this chapter that you have assimilated one of my main messages and stayed squeaky clean, that you have not in fact committed any crimes. If you have, then you are a dummy, and you will pay the price that nature exacts from dummies. You should have known that the authorities were watching you like a hawk, just waiting for you to make a slip, and you went ahead and obliged them anyway. If you are lucky you will survive the experience and you may become an asset to the Movement precisely because you have learned wisdom the hard way. I hope so. However, on to the majority of us who stay straight, use our imaginations, and hit the enemy so hard they've decided it's time to flush us.

There is a saying among Federal prosecutors: "Any second-year law student can convict a guilty man, but it takes real legal genius to convict an innocent one!" And they are right. Securing a conviction on perjury and fraudulent evidence is tricky under the best of circumstances, and they will generally assign their best forensic teams and their best FBI or BATF men to constructing the tissue of lies that will, they hope, put you away. Even that doesn't work sometimes, as witness Greensboro. The trouble is that until they can find some way to do away with the jury system completely, as they have done almost everywhere else in the world, one can never tell how a jury will react. They do their best to weed out jurors with any obvious signs of intelligence or independent thought, but the whole thing still explodes on the launching pad sometimes.

The two main weapons that have been used against the White racialist movement thus far are electronic surveillance of various kinds and the perjured testimony of informers Electronic tapes can be dubbed, spliced, re-mixed, and so on in order to have you saying things that you never uttered in your life. Videotapes are much harder to falsify and unless you're actually engaged in some kind of illegal activity they won't be used. Unless you have enough money to hire your own electronics expert to go over the prosecution's tapes and detect the splices, the re-recordings, the differences in sound level and background noise that indicate tampering, then you can be landed in deep trouble by fraudulent wiretaps and tape recordings. About the only counter to this I can suggest offhand is to be very bug-conscious. With a little bit of research you can discover how to detect electronic spying devices, how to interdict them, etc. Remember, they could be anywhere. In the presently upcoming trial of two Christian ministers for "sedition," in one case the FBI broke into the pastor's home and planted bugs in his living room. Also, you should always check your oar for bugs on a regular basis.

Informers are easier to deal with because they can be cross-examined. Since they are lying (we are, again, presuming your innocence), then they can be tripped up and their lies exposed. This also presumes that you have a genuine defense attorney who is actually interested in getting you acquitted of a bogus charge, something I'll get into momentarily. A lot of informers' testimony rests on allegations that "I was present on such-and-such a date in such-and-such a place when Bill Jones, the defendant, conspired to blow up a shopping mall." If you can prove that you were somewhere else on that date and at that time, you've got him. Now, it's very hard to remember over the intervening years and months Just where you were on the night of November the first, 1984 or whenever. You might cultivate the habit of keeping a business diary in which you record through short notations all your legitimate appointments, activities, etc. True, this may be seized and studied by the Federals in order to structure their liar's testimony around your actual schedule for the time period, but it's better than you being able to remember nothing. In general, I'd say the best preventative for this is to be an outgoing, sociable individual who spends his time in the company of others, stopping to chat with the grocery store clerk and the gas station attendant so that they will remember you being 120 miles away at the moment you were supposed to be torching some nigger church. Very general advice, I know, but each frame-up is different and it's hard to say specifically how you can protect yourself until you know the details of what you're being accused of.

In recent years, ZOG dreamed up some especially nasty little tricks that can usually put you away in double-quick time. Of these the most lethal is a bit of legal legerdemain called *fiber evidence.* The prosecution parades a bunch of professorial-type eggheads, most of whom oddly enough draw salaries or endowments from the Federal government, who will bombard a jury with all kinds of microscope slides, electronic computer analyses, textile esoterica and so on in order to prove that fibers or filaments found at the scene of a crime came from a carpet or garment in your home. This provides the crucial link which is essential for any frameup, *placing you in a particular location where in fact you were not.* You will immediately notice two things about fiber evidence. One is that it is extremely easy to forge — the eggheads might even be telling the technical truth, because they *did* find fibers from your sweater or carpet on something from the crime scene. The reason they found such fibers was that the police or FBI seized your sweater or carpet for examination and then rubbed it all over the place, on the body of the victim if any, in the room where the crime took place, so on.

The second significant aspect of fiber evidence is that it relieves the government of so much tiresome burden of proof. It is a prosecutor's dream come true. Fiber evidence relieves the district attorney's office from the nuisance of providing witnesses or concrete evidence placing you at the scene of the crime. They need not show that you were in possession of the murder or assault weapon, if any. They need not show that you were in possession of any money or goods removed from the scene. They need not show any connection at all between you and the crime other than a few microscopic filaments of textile and an earnest-sounding Yuppie or two with some fancy paper on his wall to bamboozle the jury.

Fiber evidence is in fact the last nail in the coffin of a juris principle that was one of the last bulwarks White people had against tyranny. That principle was *presumption of innocence.* Now, as most of you may have gathered by now, I am by no means a major fan of the United States Constitution. I think it is a nobly worded document of excellent intentions but then we all know what the road to hell is paved with. I think the Founding Fathers made a dog's dinner of it, to tell the truth. For one thing, it is quite obvious to anyone who knows their history and their writings that they never intended their document to apply to niggers and the new America was to be strictly Whites only, but they didn't bother to so state because it never occurred to them that any of their descendants could possibly be so imbecilic as to conceive the preposterous notion that congoids were in some way "equal" to other humanoid beings. They were otherwise brilliant men and they should have known better than to underestimate the depths which human folly and stupidity is capable of plumbing.

Be that as it may, the Constitution does have a couple of good features in it, one of these being the establishment of a judicial system based, in theory, on *presumption of innocence,* meaning that the prosecution bears the burden of proving you to be guilty of a crime rather than you being forced to prove yourself innocent, generally a much harder proposition. Fiber evidence does for presumption of innocence what Korvettenkapitän Schwieger's torpedo did for the *Lusitania.* It completely reverses the ostensible role of accuser and accused and places you in the position of explaining just how fibers from that old cardigan Mom knitted for you ten years ago got into the lace panties of a black transvestite homosexual prostitute they found beaten to death under a culvert.

Of course, you *know* how those fibers got there. The Federal secret police put them there in order to silence your political proselytizing while simultaneously discrediting you, and, by imputation, all White racists, as a perverted weirdo. How do you convince a jury of that, though? Especially a jury probably hand-picked by the prosecution to include one example of every racial enemy we've got plus a leavening of White traitors dependent on government salaries or contracts?

Here is where your lawyer, or you yourself, must shine. You are going to have to demonstrate the falsity of the government's lies, the fiber evidence, the informer's claptrap, the doctored tapes. Good luck. Here are a few very general ground rules:

1. *Never employ a lawyer who does not believe wholeheartedly in your innocence.* If he's a jaded old sot like many criminal lawyers are, or worse yet, a court-appointed attorney, he will take a purely "by-the-numbers" approach towards your case. He will do what's expected of him to earn his fee, and when they bring in the guilty verdict he'll clap you on the back and say, "Tough break, kid. If you can scrape up an extra ten G's I'll be happy to appeal this one for you." Then he heads for the handball court or an ice-cold brew at the Dew Drop Inn down the street, while niggers in uniform drag you away into living hell. Beating a fabricated Federal rap (there are few state ones) takes hard work, dedication, expense, and forensic skill. Unless your lawyer is willing to give it 110%, fire his ass and get another, or better yet, defend yourself.

2. *Defend yourself if at all possible.* Bear in mind that one of the primary purposes of a legal assault is to force you to spend money, liquidate resources, and go into debt in an effort to stay out of prison, thus diverting said funds and time and resources from the political activity the régime wants to stop. Even if you succeed in beating the rap, for that length of time they have effectively interdicted the political work of your group as all effort is channeled into your legal case. I have seen this happen time and time again. In addition, unless you have a very politically pro lawyer, you cannot rely on him to ask the right questions of the right witnesses. Remember that as a member of the bar he is technically an officer of the court and part of the System and whatever his political views, if we win he's going to be out of a job.

3. *Defend yourself properly.* Don't make a spectacle of yourself. Don't scream abuse or obscenities. Don't be disrespectful. Don't wear a uniform or other bizarre garb in court, wear a suit and tie with a neat

haircut. Don't ramble on and on. Don't interject frivolous objections. *Make that jury like you, respect you, and want to give you the benefit of the doubt and set you free.* If they're black or Judaic, try anyway. It's not a joke or a game, it's your life and your sanity that is at stake.

4. *Put the Federals on trial.* Don't let their wild assumptions and allegations go unchallenged. Question the background, qualifications, and motives of Federal witnesses minutely. Bring out the political aspect of the trial. Turn the courtroom into a forum for White nationalism, but *never lose sight of the central issue of your own innocence.* Express all political concepts or ideas *through the vehicle of your innocence.* Do all of this firmly but respectfully, forcefully but courteously. Direct half your performance towards the court reporter who is making the permanent record and half towards the jury. Make them like you and despise the 'droids in three piece suits who are trying to destroy you. Let your innocence be a constant thread that runs through the entire trial, never letting the jury lose sight of it. Never miss an opportunity to assert your innocence, but never allow yourself to become shrill or obviously bitter.

5. *Use logic and probability.* The most tightly-fashioned fabricated case will have some holes in it somewhere. Find those holes and concentrate on them, punch through and widen them until they are gaping gaps in the prosecution's case.

The law, under our system, is whatever you can make a jury believe. Remember the old saying that if you can't dazzle them with brilliance, baffle them with bullshit. Do whatever you can to make them *like* you, *dislike* the prosecutor, and introduce *doubt* into their minds. You will probably be unable to prove yourself innocent in any conclusive way unless the informer does a Perry Mason style breakdown on the stand and confesses. But if that jury goes into the deliberation room liking you, disliking the prosecutor, and smelling a definite rat in his case, then you're in with a chance. Blacks may vote to acquit you because they mistrust the System on general principles. Leftish-leaning Whites may do the same. Of course, the psychological impact on a jury varies according to the crime with which you are accused. If it's a self-defense shooting or some really tenuous case of "civil rights violation," you're in better case than if they decide to charge you with sexually molesting children.

THE ARREST

By discussing the courtroom aspect first I seem to have put the cart before the horse, but on a depressing subject like this it may be best to get the worst-case scenario over with. Actually, if you handle yourself properly during the arrest, you might not even get to court. They might decide you're too tough and sharp a cookie to risk taking on in open court where they would be bound by rules of evidence and kick you loose, telling their kosher bosses that the omens were wrong or whatever. Remember, getting caught out in a fabrication can be very embarrassing both for the D.A. and the agents involved, and they don't want to risk it unless they're sure of their ground.

Federal agents generally like to arrest you around eight o'clock in the morning, if possible dragging you away from the breakfast table in front of your family to add to the psychological humiliation and insult. Alternatively, arresting you at your workplace in order to humiliate you in front of your co-workers is a favorite method. Sometimes for dramatic effect they will get the local cops to surround the house with flak-jacketed SWAT teams and sharpshooters, thus making you out to be an extremely dangerous person. You may get cut loose twenty-four hours later for lack of evidence, but you can imagine the effect this sort of melodrama has on your neighbors, your landlord, your boss, etc.

You will note that throughout this chapter I am referring almost entirely to Federal agencies. This is because they generally are the ones who use fabrication. State and local police sometimes do so but generally lack the resources or inclination, having enough genuine crime to deal with. You must bear in mind that Federal "law enforcement" agencies, with the exception of the Secret Service which occasionally apprehends counterfeiters, all have more or less political functions as opposed to state and local agencies which deal with real crime. Most Federal offenses other than chopping firewood in a national park or such petty stuff are in some way politically useful for suppressing dissent. For instance, "mail fraud" is often used to shut down patriotic groups or others disapproved of by the régime who solicit money or sell things through the mail. Even counterfeiting can be considered a political offense, given the nature of our monetary system: they don't want private citizens printing worthless pieces of paper which compete with *their* worthless pieces of paper.

Once you are arrested you should be read your rights, and generally they will do this. It takes only a few seconds of their time, closes a possible loophole, and makes no difference whatsoever in the way they treat you. They will offer to appoint a lawyer for you before any questioning. You will not need this service, because having read this little book of mine and absorbed its lessons, you are going to *SAY NOTHING.*

You are going to say *nothing at all.* Not any time, not any where, not under any circumstances whatsoever. You will not speak to them in the car going downtown, other than to give them your name and your lawyer's name if any. You will not speak to them in the interrogation rooms. You will not speak to them in the cells. If you love your race, if you love your country, if you love your freedom and value your life and your sanity and your dignity, *YOU WILL SAY NOTHING TO THE POLICE.*

"Oh, for a Muse of fire...," wrote the immortal Shakespeare, and would that I had such a muse in order to convey to you the vital necessity of this concept. Almost anything else I have said here is open to argument or variation or experiment, except this one urgent, imperative, desperately important injunction. *Do not talk to the police!* If you do, you will pay for it with years of your life and quite possibly with your life's blood itself, spilled on the shower floor where some nigger convict has stuck a sharpened toothbrush in your gut. *Do not talk to the police!*

If you do, you may unwittingly send your friends, your loved ones, your racial brothers and sisters into living hell from which they will emerge, if ever, as shattered husks of human beings. *Do not talk to the police!* If you do, you may, with the best of intentions, and up carrying for the rest of your days the vilest stigma that can besmirch a man or woman of our race: *informer.*

I cannot count how many criminal trials I have seen or read about where the entire prosecution consisted of a couple of minor circumstantial points buttressed massively by the accused party's alleged "confession," a confession which he never intended to be such but which started as a "friendly little chat, just to get a few things in perspective." The star example of mountains of trouble coming from blabbing mouths was Greensboro. The men who were arrested immediately near the scene of the shootings were stunned, confused, upset, horrified by the whole thing. It had all been a terrible accident, couldn't the law see that? (It wasn't an "accident," the BATF set it up, but the men didn't know that.) For hour after hour they babbled into the tape recorders, getting themselves in deeper and deeper and deeper. The one man who was released, eventually, was an old pro hand at this sort of thing, Raeford Caudle, who had sense enough to let his lawyer do the talking and *kept his mouth shut.*

At the trials I can't count how many times the prosecutors waved tapes and transcripts aloft and said, "But in your initial six-hour statement to the police on November 4th, 1979 you said this, this, and that!" A good part of both major Greensboro trials consisted of the defense trying to overcome reams and reams of contradictory, self-incriminating loose talk from the men who were arrested. They couldn't understand what was happening, they were thrown for a loop by the sudden Communist attack with firearms which ATF had organized, and *they had been given no formal training by their so-called leaders in what to do when captured.* I do not except myself from this devastating indictment. I passed out a couple of procedural pamphlets and the principle of keeping silent was off-handedly discussed at a couple of meetings, but obviously the NSPA people were no better prepared than the Klan for the sudden catastrophe that overwhelmed them. You can understand now, perhaps, why I emphasize silence so much here. I have seen what hap-pens when people try to talk their way out of a jam. They just get more people involved and themselves in deeper.

The police are not your friends. In an arrest situation they are the enemy and if they try to act friendly, this is so you will relax and incriminate yourself. Remember that with a trained investigator there is no such thing as small talk. Any answer you may give him to any question at all, whether it be negative or positive, whether it seems relevant to you or not, gives him another piece to fit into the jigsaw puzzle of fabrication and falsehood that the System is building to put you away.

If torture is used on you, such as beatings or sleep deprivation or psychological mind games, then you should be prepared with some kind of story to give them when you finally can't take any more, as some people can't. The System here isn't quite as big on physical torture as they are behind the Iron Curtain; generally nigger prison inmates are employed to punish or soften up White suspects, so the Feds don't have to get their hands dirty or blood all over their Gucci shoes. The System's specialty is psychological and mental torture. They will Mutt-and-Jeff you where one cop is the heavy and one is the decent Joe who wants to help you and thinks you're getting a raw deal. They will hold out the prospect of release with little lines like, "Come on, Ed, let's get this cleared up and put to bed so we can all go home, OK?", implying that if you confess you will somehow miraculously be allowed to go home.

They will speak to you calmly, reasonably, and then suddenly jump up and start screaming obscenities and accusations at you in order to shock and disorient you. They will bring in the biggest nigger on their force and threaten to let him beat you or sodomize you if you do not confess; alternatively they will threaten to put you into a cell overnight with one or more nigger homosexuals, There have been cases where this was actually done and our people have been badly hurt trying to resist mass anal gang-rape. I generally don't make comments like this, but I want to put all present law-enforcement people on notice that after the revolution, any former cop or FBI agent found guilty of aiding or abetting any kind of prison assault on Whites has bought himself a one-way ticket to the gallows. If I don't make it, I think my successors who do will agree with this policy. That's not a threat, guys. It's a promise. You sent our leaders to Nuremberg and thereby set a precedent; turn-about will be fair play.

If you lose your case, you will be sent to prison. I have been lucky so far. I have faced the enemy courts on a serious charge only once and in that case my deportation order from the country in question took precedence and my jail term was suspended. I have had a few more minor scrapes but never gone to one of these hellish places ZOG maintains as the final, ultimate deterrent. I am therefore not qualified to try and teach you how to survive in such an inferno. I admit that the prospect terrifies me; sometimes I wake up at night in a cold sweat from nightmares about some American prison. So far I have not let this threat deter me from doing my duty, and in this the prison menace has failed its masters. I hope that if and when the time comes I will be able to face it without betraying myself and my people, but since I have yet to face that test, I can't very well tell others how to face it.

I have but one comment to make about the whole prison scenario, and that is that I know it *can be done,* it can be survived, because I have known those who have done so. Robert Miles survived it, and even as I write he faces yet another term for "sedition" with calm courage and a dignity that elevates his cause and ours into greatness. Leroy Gibson survived it, and came out of Atlanta swinging. The Gerhardt brothers survived it. Jim Mason survived it, Robert Shelton and J.B. Stoner and Jack Fowler and a host of others survived it. In the cases of these men I have mentioned and many more, the system did its worst and it failed. It tried to destroy them and instead strengthened their faith and hardened their spirit for the struggle. The System can be beaten, brothers. The comrades I have named and every other White man who has come out of prison with his honor and his pride intact have beaten it. Some day we will beat it down.

A word on deals: don't. Don't make deals with the cops. Don't make deals with the courts to cop a plea. Never plead guilty to anything. The reason for this is simple: ZOG is a liar and anything its servants tell you cannot be trusted. If you make a deal, it may suit ZOG's Byzantine purposes to keep its part of the bargain. Then again, it may not. Probably not. The prisons are full of men who could have sworn they had a "deal" with ZOG. ZOG doesn't deal, it uses, it consumes, and it throws people aside. Do not put your trust in any judge, any lawyer, or any law officer. They are there for one purpose: to suppress any dissenting or unorthodox thoughts you may have in your head and to ensure you remain a productive labor unit, keeping the System's creaky old machinery going and footing the bill like honkies are supposed to. If you are no longer salvageable as a labor unit, then you must be scrapped.

A final word: train your family and comrades to be silent as well, especially to the media following your arrest. One of the most excruciatingly embarrassing episodes in the whole Greensboro fiasco was when a bunch of sappy women were discovered by some reporters visiting their male relatives in Jail. These ladies proceeded to babble on and on about how racism wasn't Christian and them horrible Klan and Nazi fellers jeet plain lured Lucius astray, and we all just *loves* colored folks and Jesus is a-gonna come and split the sky open and we's all gonna be *raptured* and fly up to meet Jesus in the sky 'ceptin fer Klan and Nazis who was goin' to hell and Lucius was down on his knees in his cell prayin' fer the souls of them horrible racists that they might see the light and repent blah, blah, blah, on and on and on! This was really the sort of thing those men in jail needed to boost their morale right at that moment!

A loose comment to a reporter or cop by a wife, husband, relative, or friend can get the jailed comrade ten to twenty if it's the wrong thing to say. All family members should be instilled right from the beginning with the primary directive: *don't talk to the police!* You should have a set procedure for what is to be done if your house is searched, if you are arrested, if you are charged. You should know a bail bondsman or someone willing to put up bail for you, to save frantic leafing through the Yellow Pages on the day. Your wife or husband should be just as conversant as you are in your legal rights. He or she should demand to see warrants and *read them* before allowing a search, and demand a receipt for anything taken. And remember: *don't talk to the police!*

IX.
MOVEMENT FINANCES

Sometimes people ask me when the great White revolution is going to occur. I tell them, "Whenever you and enough people like you are willing to foot the bill for it!" I am not referring solely to money, but to a good degree I am speaking literally when I say that. Revolution comes with one hell of a price tag. The first thing you will learn when you begin your political activism is the crucially vital importance of money. *Someone must pay.* Revolution nowadays is big business. The days when something might be accomplished by a handful of conspirators whispering around a guttering candle in a deserted Gothic ruin at midnight are long gone. Revolution demands organization, manpower, political analysis of the keenest type, ruthless discipline, skilful propaganda, and above all, massive financing.

This money does not simply drop out of the skies. It must be obtained from a variety of sources. *Someone must pay.* And the simple fact is that the major source of all racial nationalist financing has always been, and will continue to be, the White working people who make up the vast majority of every organization's membership and peripheral support. In other words, the people who can least afford it must shoulder the biggest part of the burden. This is grossly unfair, and worse than that, it is also inefficient and a very poor way of financing our cause. But to be frank, I'm damned if I can see any *realistic* way out of this impasse in the near future. To tell you why is going to take some explaining.

In order to discover the root causes of this Movement's perpetual poverty, we must look closely at the whole nature of what we're doing and who we are. Remember the big lefty "revolution" of the late 1960s? the hippies, the yippies, the Berkeley Free Speech Movement, the Weathermen, that whole scene where everybody was going to tune in, turn on, drop out, off the pigs, and so on? That big left-wing "Power to the People" revolution that was going to overthrow the military-industrial complex and create an Age of Aquarius where everybody sat around on the grass smoking dope while listening to Jimi Hendrix and ran around naked fornicating with everything that moved? The leadership of this mess was Jewish, of course, the Rudds and Hoffmans and Rubins, but what about all those White hippie-dippy types who were going to do all this guff?

A couple of things happened. First off, there was Kent State and the University of Wisconsin bombing, and little rich Weathergirl Diana Oughton blew her pampered alabaster ass into hamburger in a townhouse in New York. Diana was down in the basement making bombs and she must have touched the wrong wires together, because she leveled some prominent hebe lawyer's house and took two of her Weatherperson companions with her, in addition to literally blowing the socks off another couple of Weatherbimbi who ran next door stark naked and literally smoking from the blast, asking if they could come in and use the shower. Their friends, you will note, had just vaporized themselves through their own stupidity and the cops were on the way, and yet the first reaction of the surviving pair was to get all that nasty proletarian dirt cleaned off. In this little anecdote one sees the whole story of the so-called New Left. The reason they never got anywhere serious was that they were not revolutionaries. They were *poseurs,* spoiled rich kids playing Che Guevera. During that spring and summer of 1970, all of a sudden it wasn't a game anymore, and it finally dawned on the stupid jerks that you could get *killed* playing revolutionary. A few diehards hung onto the pose for a couple of years, but most of them saw the light very quickly indeed. The opening of the academic year in September 1970 was noticeably sedate.

The affluent urban guerrillas of the Sixties were never short of bail money, never had to work for their livings, and could afford all manner of books, drug paraphernalia and drugs, pre-shrunk and factory-discolored jeans that let them imitate real workers, all the material they needed for their picket signs and underground newspapers, etc. Mommy and Daddy picked up the tab and gave them a good steak-and-potatoes feed when they went home to suburbia to get a break from the brown rice and ginseng tea at the revolutionary consciousness-raising communes or whatever.

One of the most hysterically funny things I have ever read is the story of how the Weathermen tried to enlist the aid of the "grease," as they contemptuously referred to the White blue-collar kids of Detroit and Chicago. They went out to the local burger doodle and harangued these youngsters where they hung out, passing out Marxist tracts and urging them to come to Chicago for their "Days of Rage." On one occasion a group of crazed Weatherwomen charged into a high school and ran up and down the corridors screaming "Jailbreak!" and smashing windows. They were thrown out on their denim-clad derrieres by the varsity football squad.

Those poor, working-class White kids may not have had much use for the police or authority, but you weren't going to catch *them* going down to Chicago and deliberately attacking the law and getting themselves busted. Precisely because they came from the real world of brute labor and poverty, they knew better. They had no rich Daddies to come and bail them out when they got thrown in the can; they had to sit there for months on end subsisting on swill and fighting off the nigger rapists. It is precisely those kids whom the Reds so arrogantly called "the grease" who form the nucleus of every White racial nationalist organization. Unlike the Left, which is composed of white middle-class race traitors, Jews, and non-Whites, our Movement is genuinely based in the working class. One of the best descriptions I ever heard of November 3rd, 1979 in Greensboro was, "The Communist Worker's Party finally met some workers."

COMPREHENSION: White racial nationalism is the genuine dissent in this society, the only real heresy which is persecuted in an attempt to destroy it. Our people are this society's scapegoats, the heretics who must be burned at the stake before we can contaminate others with our dangerous thoughts.

The Left enrolls teachers, lawyers, doctors, university professors, writers, actors, social workers, Yuppies, ministers and priests, professional "community activists" who are adept at getting government paychecks and funding from tax dollars. The conservative right has a somewhat similar make-up with a healthy injection of funds from the business community and multi-nationals, but then conservatives are only interested in preserving their money and not their race, and do not fall within the purview of this book. They are part of the problem, not part of the solution, Our people, however, are men who work with their hands and women who bear and raise children. In the ranks of the Klan or the National Socialist groups or the Identity churches, you will find electricians and plumbers, auto mechanics and television repairmen, farmers and bricklayers, truck drivers and short order cooks, nurses and beauticians, small business owners and construction workers, secretaries and waitresses, as well as many older comrades who can remember a better way of life and want to help us return to it.

Nothing else than this dichotomy of membership so ably illustrates the bona fide revolutionary nature of the Movement. Unfortunately, it not only means that our people have little to contribute to the coffers themselves, but that they live their lives so far removed from the financial fountainheads, the levers of power that make money flow, that they are unable to tap into major sources of funding like the Left can. Reds can always get money from governments, either our government or assorted foreign ones. They have refined the art of getting their grubby little paws on taxpayers' dollars to unbelievable degrees of subtlety. The Left can batten onto White liberal churches and religious groups with practiced ease. Their members are conversant with every free handout both private and public going anywhere, and slurp away at the trough just like ZOG's bigger swine. Look closely enough and you will discover that virtually every major left-wing cause for the past thirty years has been financed by taxpayers' money to a greater or lesser degree.

What does all this mean in a pragmatic sense? It means that from the word go you will be perpetually short of money. You will need funds for printing equipment, paper, graphic supplies, gasoline for political transportation, office space, recorded telephone messages, political campaigns, advertising, filing fees for candidates, bail money for arrested comrades, legal fees, telephone bills, rent on necessary facilities, security equipment, electronic gear for making videos and cassettes, computers and their accessories. The list folds out on and on. The story of your political work will be one long, desperate, urgent search for funding, the quest for just a few paltry dollars for this or that will occupy the bulk of your time, and your mailing list will groan under the constant bombardment of incessant fund appeals. "What? Asking for more money? I just *gave* ten dollars last month. What happened to that?" You will be amazed at the miracles your supporters expect you to perform with their five or ten dollar intermittent donations, and you will be even more amazed at the miracles you *do* perform with so little.

I will discuss fund-raising techniques in a bit, but there is one thing I want to warn you about, and that is that when all is said and done *there is no substitute for direct donation* as a means of financing the WRP. You must succeed in conveying this to your supporters, because if you don't, then after a while they are going to get the idea that you regard them as mere teats to be milked, which is in fact the case with many of the fraudulent "patriot for profit" groups. You must always let your supporters know that you value them and that by contributing they are doing their bit for the race. One little tip I will give you right now that will increase your income by 50% in itself: *always answer your mail.* Answer it even if there is no donation enclosed but most especially if there is. Nothing irritates and angers people more than sending a donation they might have used for other purposes to a political group on the understanding that it will go towards the common cause, and never getting any kind of acknowledgement. Always acknowledge dues as well, although dues imply formalized membership and in my view that's something that shouldn't exist.

Before I discuss actual fund-raising I want to talk about two methods that we nasty racist types are constantly being accused of using, and another that our friends and supporters often urge us to use in order to relieve them of the annoyance of constant fund appeals.

The first source of money that we are all supposed to draw on according to the enemy media and propagandists is that mythological creature, the *right-wing fat cat.* Supposedly there is a cabal of multi-millionaires who have nothing better to do with all their moola than lavish it in buckets on every right-wing and racist cause that comes along. The media and slanderers always imply that there is something really sinister going on here, some kind of hidden agenda, and every racial nationalist and rightish organization is part of some worldwide ongoing conspiracy. The Jews especially get very paranoid about these mysterious right-wing fat cats and their conspiracies. (Understandably so, since the Jews of all people know the power of secret conspiracy as a force in world affairs.)

I have been in the White racial resistance in one form or another for nineteen years, since 1 was thrown into an integrated high school two weeks short of my fifteenth birthday. During all that time I have only once gotten any genuine, definite glimpse of these so-called "fat cats." There have been a few moderately well-to-do people of the upper middle class who have dabbled in racial nationalist politics as a sort of hobby hut I find that most of these people don't last more than a year or so before the hobby gets too expensive and too dangerous for their taste. There are a small handful of noble and notable exceptions. Virtually every racialist leader has a couple of quiet backers that he can generally rely upon for a couple of hundred bucks in an *emergency;* if he is wise he only calls on these people when the chips are really down lest he kill the golden goose, so to speak. But no more than a couple of hundred. I received thousand-dollar donations on three occasions, as I recall, during my entire five year tenure with the NSPA, and these were all from one man who had been lucky enough to land a good medium-term contract in his business.

Just *once,* I may have gotten close to the big bucks. In the autumn of 1980 I was approached by intermediaries who conveyed to me a series of conditions involving the strategic and tactical nature of the NSPA and asking certain specific changes be made in the way we were proceeding. In exchange for bringing the party into line with these conditions, which I might add were nothing any genuine White racial patriot couldn't live with, I was offered a financial package that would have put us on an equal footing with both the Republican and Democratic machines in the state of North Carolina. The offer was withdrawn when the events of December 1980 became known and when other events took place between the new year and the first day of April when I resigned.

I don't want to go into details, because it is my fondest hope that someday these same people may be approachable. But I need to point out that this tentative contact was made *because the NSPA was showing results.* Wealthy people became wealthy because they are smart with their money and know a good investment when they see it. It is up to us to prove that we are a good investment in the future. When we can demonstrate maturity, efficiency, dedication, quality personnel, and above all *start showing results,* then the big money will find us. Rich people may occasionally be willing to spend a little on the present Movement as a hobby, but not much. They are willing to subsidize strength, but refuse to prop up weakness, and rightly so. The fact is that most present racial nationalist groups don't deserve major financing and wouldn't know what to do with it if they got it.

In addition, I am citing my own experience to underline an important thing for all of you to remember. Without going into a long re-hash of the past, I am convinced that the destruction of the NSPA between December 1980 and April of 1981 was part of a deliberately orchestrated plot involving at least two government agencies. This was virtually admitted to me by the U.S. Attorney in New Orleans in June of that year when I was down there dodging another one of their assassination attempts. Big Brother knows very well that money is the key to our potential success, and once any group starts showing signs of being adequately financed or being about to come into big money, then the subversion and quasi-legal fabrication machine will go into high gear. When you get going strong and the support starts rolling in and green starts falling out of the envelopes in your mail, be very, very careful. ZOG will notice and ZOG will attack. Make sure he has nothing to sink his rotting fangs into.

The second fund-raiser that the media periodically accuse us of being adept in is *expropriation,* or armed robbery. Proper political expropriation is a legitimate revolutionary tool and various Communist groups use it routinely around the world. I should make it clear that by expropriation I do not mean theft, which in our sense means stealing from White working people, robbing Mom and Pop stores, holding up franchise stores or burger doodles where the take is derisory and White employees are endangered, burglarizing White homes, this kind of thing. Stealing from White working class families and individuals is not only disgraceful, it's stupid. Our people have very little to steal anymore; they live from paycheck to paycheck and are mortgaged up to the hilt. Expropriation, in the White sense, means seizing a portion of the wealth which has been stolen from White people and returning it to our race through the medium of the resistance. Banks, insurance companies, loansharks, any government body, Jews, racetracks and porno shops, supermarket chains, everyone who rips our people off and grows fat and bloated on those obscene profits, these ought to be the target of White revolutionary expropriation.

The benevolent outlaw who is the champion of the downtrodden and who avenges the poor and weak against the wealthy and the strong is a common folk hero among Aryan man, although significantly no similar character appears anywhere in the Semitic world. The English have Robin Hood, the prototype of the chivalrous outlaw; the Americans have Jesse James and his Colt Dragoons; the Germans have Schinderhannes of the Rhine, whose favorite target was a nice fat Jewish tax collector; the Italians have their banditti, and the Irish their highwayman Willie Brennan. Both common sense and our own rich racial history and culture teach us that there is nothing *morally* wrong with taking back a modicum of our own stolen wealth from the thieves who appropriated it in the first place. But is it *wise* to do so at this point in time? Is it practical? Is it likely to advance our cause?

I won't bother to repeat my usual injunctions to stay legal; if you haven't gotten the message by now you aren't going to get it. But I feel I must emphasize here that legality is *a tactic,* not some kind of moral absolute. It is true that the Washington régime has the law on its side, but then tyrants always do. Their monopoly of the law is what distinguishes tyrants from ordinary thieves and murderers. I advise against expropriation during the first three phases of the White revolutionary struggle on purely practical grounds. There is no point in robbing $50,000 from a bank if no good will come to the cause from the money because you and your entire group are in jail. Bear in mind that if there are ten of you and two commit a crime, any crime, the pair will go down for the offense itself and the other eight for "conspiracy," a legalistic nonsense that can mean whatever ZOG wants it to mean, just like the equally meaningless "violation of civil rights." Plus, if a White racialist group gets caught pulling a robbery it reinforces the enemy propaganda stereotype that we are criminals. We need serious revolutionary politics, not a Monty Python suicide squad that runs out and disembowels itself.

The final fund-raising method that has often been suggested is the idea of White racist businesses or entrepreneurial projects designed to raise money for the cause and relieve the people on the mailing list of the constant begging fund appeals. This has in fact been tried to some extent, rather along the lines of the White economic co-op idea I discussed earlier. It has had some middling success in cushioning our people against the effects of Judaic economic warfare and defunctionalization, but as far as actually raising any large amounts of money for purely political use goes, the results have been decidedly mixed. I do not rule out some sort of association or fraternity of White businessmen who are already in place with viable enterprises, but I am not sanguine about the concept as a long-range source of the type of massive financing any political group must have.

The problem is that the whole economic structure of Western society is slanted against the individual entrepreneur and small businessman, however much the conservative monetarists may hymn the Mom and Pop shop. I found this out the hard way when I tried to establish my own business in Ireland, which is admittedly the Mississippi of Europe, but the same conditions prevail elsewhere. Unless the would-be Rockefeller lucks onto a huge amount of capital for initial set-up costs, he is going to start out in hock up to his eyeballs to the bank. That is presuming he can get a loan at all, which is getting harder and harder from what I read in the business sections of most newspapers. The problem is that unless you are really on the ball and identify some need that the big boys in your field aren't supplying, whatever you do can be done better and whatever you sell can be bought cheaper at the K-Mart, Sears & Roebuck, Safeway, etc.

Even if you do happen onto some previously overlooked angle, you can bet that once you have demonstrated the profitability of the product or service, the big multi-nationals will find a way to eliminate you, either buying you out for a derisory fraction of what your idea is worth or brutally running you out of business if you refuse to play ball. It happens every day. One thing Yehudi does know how to do is to bring home that shekel. Personally, I think we would be fools to try and compete with the Jews in their own area of expertise. This is war, and Hannibal's first rule of warfare was never to fight the enemy on ground of his own choosing.

Once the political business is established, you will find that more and more of your time, personnel, money, and effort go into keeping the business afloat as you try to compete with older, better established outfits. Correspondingly less of said time, effort, etc., go into the political work the business was ostensibly set up to fund. You may recall the little sign one sees in various offices: "When you're up to your ass in alligators, it is difficult to recall that your original objective was to drain the swamp." And once the yids find out who's behind Papa A's Kosher Barbecue or Eichmann & Sons Quality Lampshades, then they will proceed to do that voodoo the Jew do so well. You will find yourself sans customers, harassed on the tax and legal fronts, and in Chapter 11 bankruptcy court before you can say "Oy gevalt!"

Think it can't happen to you? The System got the multi-million dollar PTL television empire eventually, and PTL wasn't even political, the hebes just got nervous at the competition on the silver screen.

You must bear in mind that one of the major strategies that the enemy has used against us for generations is aimed specifically at eliminating a certain type of individual within the White community, who may be loosely designated as the *yeoman* or freeholder. The German *bauer,* the Russian *kulak,* the Irish "strong farmer" would be good analogies. These are White men, generally of middle years, who are married and actually function as the head of their nuclear family units, while the wife and mother is the heart. They own their own source of sustenance, their own land and tools or in the modern equivalency their own shops and inventories. Also included in this category should be independent artisans who again own their own tools and sell their skills to their fellow Whites in the community. This is anathema to ZOG, who wants us all selling our labor and our skills to the System for wages and thus become dependent on the status quo for our survival.

White yeoman types are dangerous to ZOG for other reasons. They often own their own weapons, are familiar with their use and have had military training, in many cases serving in the reserves or the militia. They tend to be politically participatory, and that is a definite no-no for us honkies: politics is for lawyers and other favored Yuppies and we mustn't get ideas above our station. An independent source of income leads to disturbingly independent thoughts and deeds. It is no coincidence that William Tell was a yeoman farmer of the high Swiss mountains, and that when he came into town it was there that he refused to salute the Jew Gessler's cap on the pole in the square. In consequence, Tell had to shoot the apple off his son's head using the crossbow he was such a dead shot with from his free Aryan life in the mountain fastnesses. Afterwards he used the same crossbow to shoot some things off Gessler and his Austrian mercenaries. (Yes, even in the Middle Ages there were Whites who sold their sword arms to Judah for gold.)

Under the present conditions and in the existing economic climate, any attempt at starting a small business is going to be a very dicey undertaking at best. By all means, experiment with it. Maybe we just haven't found the right formula yet. Just always bear in mind that your original objective is to drain the swamp, i.e., the business should support racial nationalist political activity and not vice versa. We are not businessmen and we are not in this to make a living, marginal or comfortable. We are in this thing to change the world and ensure that ten thousand years from now there are still some William Tells around who will refuse to salute Gessler's cap and will be just as dab a hand with a plutonium death ray as he was with a crossbow.

Getting back to our original subject after all this historical and philosophic digression, the fact remains that you can't always be hitting up your small handful of faithful supporters for operating funds. Morale and personal considerations aside, the fact is that they can't afford it. There are a number of techniques that you can use to widen the circle of your support. If you are able to publish a small newsletter of some kind, by all means charge a subscription rate to out-of-staters and other inactives. Most of them are hobbyists who will read your newsletter and then throw it into the closet along with a couple of tons of other such material that they have accumulated since 1971. Never tolerate deadbeats on your mailing list. Cull those who do not respond regularly and don't let your list get cluttered up with people you haven't heard from for three years, non-paying prisoners, obvious lunatics who write you bizarre letters of the pardon-the-crayon-they-don't-let-us-have-any-thing-sharp-here variety. Your newsletter and your mailing list are functional tools and like all tools should be serviced regularly and kept in good condition.

However, a sign of health and vigor in any organization is that the bulk of its funding comes from local sources. This is important for several reasons. First off, it is by no means impossible that eventually ZOG may get around to some kind of official postal censorship, classing "racist literature" along with pornography as unlawful to send through the mails. Secondly, your primary function is supposed to be organizing in your own area, not pinching five and ten buck donations from people who might otherwise be helping out the WRP or activity unit in their own areas. It is especially uncool to poach donations from another unit of your own party, and can lead to unnecessary tension and aggro.

Finally, without intending it to happen this way, publishing a newsletter or newspaper or journal can lead to other things like selling books and pamphlets through the mail, then selling Third Reich regalia and other toys, and then all of a sudden you're a book peddler instead of a revolutionary. Let me make it clear that there are a number of good publishers and book dealers in the Movement who are performing an invaluable service to us all, and I certainly do not mean to imply any criticism of them. But this book is not aimed at the publisher or bookseller, it is meant to instruct and encourage activists. If you decide from the beginning that your contribution to our racial struggle is going to be the provision of agitational and educational material, job printing, a quality magazine or newsletter, then fine. But don't fall into books and mail-order peddling out of laziness, as a "safe" way of helping in the struggle without risk. (Or so you may think. Our publishers and book dealers get attacked and burned out too, as witness the torching of the Institute for Historical Review.)

Every man and woman in your unit should be a twenty-four hour fund raiser for the organization. There are manuals written for voluntary service groups like the United Way on how to raise money, and you need to get hold of a few of these pamphlets and try to adapt their ideas to your needs. Try all the old standards like yard sales, collecting beer cans for aluminum recycling, scrap copper and brass for sale to private yards. Sell homegrown fruit and vegetables at roadside stands or door to door. Hold fund-raising barbecues and dinners wherein the food is contributed and with a five or ten dollars a plate cover charge. Operate a literature room or other facility where White racial nationalist literature is sold at a reasonable mark-up; I might add that you can put together an extensive list of books and publications put out by System publishers which are ideologically *linientreu* and which can be sold in any flea market or book fair. These would include books on Norse mythology, European culture and history, older books about American history that haven't been tampered with by the Jews and the liberal-left re-writers of our heritage; older children's books that haven't been filled with nigger and Chinese kiddies seeing Spot run and so on; gun magazines, Third Reich memorabilia such as post cards and other small items; certain works of science fiction; used cassettes and LPs of Aryan music, etc.

If you can find a way to obtain government funding in some guise, by all means do so. Collect every pamphlet, publication, and book you can find about government benefits and freebies. The left-wing press is a mine of information about things applicable to our financial problems, so study it. You need to know the enemy and know whatever he can teach us. Look for lists of government auctions where you can often buy everything from a typewriter to a two and a half-ton truck, reams of copying paper to surplus field jackets. If there is some freebie going to any absurd minority who applies, then by all means put in your own application as a spokesman for your city's Orthodox Basque community. (No kidding—I once got a job on an affirmative action quota by listing myself as a "polygamous Mormon"!) I also have heard of Whites obtaining food stamps and affirmative action jobs by blatantly claiming to be black or Indian, and under their own regulations the Feds had to take their word for it!

There are some racial patriots who believe that "sponging" off the government is shameful and Whites should be too proud to do it. The way I look at it, it's your money, so why shouldn't you get some of it back? Otherwise they'll just give it to niggers.

A few words about fund-raising through the mail: *watch potential mail fraud.* This is a favorite device ZOG likes to use. If someone orders a book or something from your mail order service, take their money and then *send them what they ordered,* by return mail if possible. One well-known patriot for profit tried selling "Victory Bonds" to be repaid with interest within one year after his party took power. He almost got canned for Federal mail fraud and a state bunco charge as well; at the last minute the charges were mysteriously dropped, something I personally believe was due to his ADL protectors intervening on his behalf because he was doing good work for them where he was. Never try to sell anything intangible by mail. Reverend Ike can get away with it; we can't. Also watch your tax situation. Collect and pay all applicable sales tax on time. Keep straight with the IRS, for God's sake.

Be open about money with the trusted people in your unit. Keep books and let anyone who cares to inspect them, so long as you know the individual's interest is a loyal one. In any case, to be perfectly frank, you won't have all that much to conceal for a good while. Most of your donations will be small and you will immediately spend what comes in on necessary goods and services. Watch your own lifestyle. Even if you make a pretty good buck, if people see you driving a Cadillac and living it up they will draw their own conclusions. Nothing can so divide and hamper a White racial organization than doubts about the way money is being spent. As a potential leader of our race during the terrible times to come, one of the first things you must prove to your own people is that you can be trusted. If your comrades know that they can trust you with a couple of bucks, then they will come to know that they can trust you with their lives. Don't betray that trust. Make sure that every cent you receive for political purposes is spent, one way or another, on something political or racial.

The money problem will never go away. As the base of our support grows and those five, ten, and twenty dollar contributions mount up, the expenses will also increase accordingly. Right up to the very day of victory we are still going to be passing the hat, to our own people, to business cartels, to foreign governments, to anyone who will stump up a bit of green. Accept it, become used to it, and learn to work around the situation. If our White revolutionaries are a tank crew and our faith and dedication is a tank, then money is the precious petrol or diesel fuel that keeps the tank running. You should never be ashamed to ask for that life-giving essence. Fund-raising is part of your job and you should never be reticent about it. I never have been — ask my supporters!

ELECTIONS

The first thing you must realize about elections is that they are all fraudulent. They are bogus in one of two ways: either the votes are not counted honestly and correctly, or else the office to which the individual attains election exercises no genuine power in the sense that the elected official can initiate actual change. Our society is not run by elected officials but by bureaucrats and invisible cabals whose existence is only vaguely suspected by the general public. In some cases both types of falsity pertain to an election or an elective office. In any case, if the office is one of the few that *do* exercise any genuine power, you can be certain that the results are always predetermined. Elections are fraudulent in the larger sense that almost never is any genuine choice offered to the voters. It is Tweedledum the Democrat and Tweedledee the Republican in nine cases out of ten. I do see some signs that a slight degree of bona fide differentiation is beginning to creep into the ossified American political system, but this consists merely in the alignment of special interest groups with one or the other of the two major parties. Broadly speaking, the growing non-White and sexually perverted elements are trying to co-opt the Democrats and the old-line big money interests as well as the powerful religious racketeers of television have successfully co-opted the Republican party. There is no place for the White working man in either of these special-interest factions.

Finally, in any case it is neither the legislative nor the executive branches of government which exercise the ultimate governing power in America, but the judiciary.

Insofar as actual governance does take place, it is this small clique of several thousand appointed functionaries, drawn without exception from the moneyed élite or the privileged non-White auxiliary races, which commands in our society. It is this fact which makes running in elections an ultimately pointless exercise for White racial nationalists. Even if we *did* win an election, the ADL or some liberal group would simply run huffing and puffing to the nearest Federal judge as fast as their bandy little legs would carry them. An injunction would be issued to prevent our man from taking office and some quasi-legal fiction found or invented to void the election results.

So should we even bother? The answer is yes, definitely. Our ultimate goal in pursuing elected office should be precisely the one I have just mentioned, that of winning and *forcing the enemy to break his own rules* in order to prevent us from getting anywhere near the reins of power, Bear in mind that huge areas of this country outside the major cities are still predominantly White and it is by no means beyond the bounds of possibility that we could eventually fight and win elections, presuming the votes were counted honestly. By forcing the enemy into election fraud or perversion of the law in order to defeat us, we are in fact defeating him, if you can see my meaning.

One of our primary tasks must be to destroy the small remaining faith that White Americans place in the System. One of their few remaining illusions is that if something really gets too unbearable, then they can somehow just vote it away. White Americans still cling to their precious ballot box like a life preserver despite constantly accumulating evidence that the elections are rigged. If we can destroy that naive, childish belief in the power of their puny little vote, then they will be ripe for us.

COMPREHENSION: White revolution will be won when we master the skill of fighting the System with a ballot paper in one hand and a rifle in the other.

Elections serve other invaluable purposes. They provide a legitimate forum where we can air our program and our views. They result in White candidates getting opportunities to speak which would otherwise be denied to them, and to reach audiences through media coverage that it would take hundreds of thousands of dollars to reach otherwise. Elections also generate a type of negative but still helpful publicity in that the presence of a White candidate on a ballot will send the local liberals and hebes into a screaming rage *and* cause them to denounce us hysterically and curse any White who dares to vote for us, thus showing us up in relief and giving the White community a good perspective. Remember, we will be known not only by what we say but by who our enemies are and what *they* say about us. A large part of successful revolutionary agitation consists of provoking the enemy into overreaction.

Elections are also a spur to fund-raising and recruitment. Like it or not, most White Americans have been conditioned from birth to think of politics in terms of elections, and with the limited resources at our command it is going to be a long time before we can get them thinking in terms of *Gleichschaltung* or political totality of life. They will respond to an election campaign better than most types of "missionary" work because it expresses White nationalism in their limited frame of political reference.

When fighting an election campaign, you need to have a viable candidate first. He or she should be intelligent, articulate, and devoid of obvious physical deformity as modern-day politics consists almost entirely of image. The candidate should have no skeletons in his or her closet, since you can bet your bippy that the news media are going to dig, and dig deep. Indeed, having a candidate with no previous history of dishonesty, crime, or perversion will give us an edge on most System candidates from the very beginning. It is also a good idea if the candidate is someone who is either immune or only marginally vulnerable to defunctionalization and economic retaliation, although sometimes this isn't practical.

It is always best to form a "Henry Higgins for State Senate" committee, a specific front group with the purpose of running this one candidate's campaign. This is because most states have election laws requiring political action committees to file reports of election expenses and contributions, one of those absurd body of regulations that System candidates ignore at will but which can be used to trip up the unwary and unapproved candidacy. Form your committee, get all the paperwork from your state or local board of elections, fill everything out in triplicate, and then dissolve your committee after the election so as to leave a minimum paper trail.

You will generally find that below a certain amount, say $25, you are not required to list the name and address of contributors. Make sure all your donations are below this limit. Under no circumstances hand over to the government any list of names and addresses of supporters, other than ones you already know have been identified or those with whom you have discussed this beforehand and agree to allow their names to be used. A whole report with nothing but five and ten dollar contributions listed is going to look suspicious, so it is as well to have some already-known names listed. Bear in mind that these reports are a matter of public record and if you list financial contributors, then you are targeting these people for victimization. Anyone can get a copy of your report— the media, the JDL, anyone. This is, of course, breaking the law. However, you must decide which is more heinous violating a System law designed to hamper and suppress meaningful political dissent, or handing over the name of a friend and comrade to people who may get him fired, maim him with a bomb, or murder him. The choice is a simple and moral one. I shouldn't have to tell you which alternative you must take.

Am I contradicting myself here on the legality question? Mayhap, a wee bit. But just as pure survival can countermand the legality dictum, there is also a higher law than that of man which must on occasion be taken into account. I have said that the primary purpose of legality is as a tactic to ensure *survival.* However, it means survival with a purpose, survival as a moral White Aryan human being. Any rat or cockroach can merely continue to exist. Our task is harder. We must continue to exist and function as *spiritual and moral emissaries to the rest of our race.* That means that there are times when we must take the ethical high ground no matter what the cost. One of the most deeply rooted principles by which we must live is that one simply does not betray a comrade to ZOG. Never. Not under any circumstances.

Getting back to elections, all printing and expenditure which is undertaken in support of the candidate should be done by the official committee for his or her election. The campaign literature and program should reflect the WRP's policy in all things. For this reason it is important to select the offices for which your candidates run with care. The office should be such that the WRP's program can in fact be adapted to fit the needs and local conditions surrounding that office and its function.

The key to selecting an office for which to run is, indeed, the adaptability of that office to the White revolutionary program. With rare exceptions, small local offices, such as dogcatcher in Frostbite, Vermont or Inspector of Public Sanitary Facilities in Hog Wallow, Arkansas are pointless to try for. So are most local city council and county commissioner seats. These bodies are not truly political, they are administrative, concerning themselves with sewers and street lights and the logistics of community planning and services. It is very difficult to introduce issues of a wide-ranging and national-level importance into a discussion on bond issues for a new bus garage or water treatment plant. In larger cities like Chicago or Boston the city council does in fact wield power, wealth, and influence, and these seats are worth attempting. You will always be fighting established municipal machines and sometimes this can get very dirty. Remember what was said in Chapter One about System thieves who see their incomes and their power threatened. In big cities the back-room boys can play rough, so be prepared.

One good office, though, is the local board of education in almost any town or city of any size. If you have a candidate who is a parent of children themselves, this is an excellent possibility and should be explored. Women candidates especially are good for board of education races, and if elected can have a direct influence on the behavior of staff and administrators in the schools, the textbooks used, the degree of left-wing and liberal and sexually perverted indoctrination, etc.

I personally would recommend avoiding state legislatures, unless you have a very good grass roots constituency group in a particular district and you're able to try it as a sort of saturation exercise, hitting the neighborhoods and towns in the district over and over again and using the media to blitz the operational area. But state legislatures are mostly boring talking shops, running the sewers and roads and street lights just like city councils except on a larger scale, wasting time in somnolent committees and providing pork barrel money and jobs for the boys.

The offices to go for are state-wide ones where your White racial candidate's name will be on the ballot throughout the entire state, thus increasing the vote proportionally. Even if you only get (or are only allowed) 2% of the vote, the 30,000 votes you rack up in a state-wide race look a lot better for propaganda purposes than the 300 you'd show in a municipal election. Federal offices are generally going to be out of our league expense-wise, but then again if you can see an opening there and you have the manpower and the money to take on the task, by all means go for it. Nothing ventured, Nothing gained.

XI.
THE POLITICS OF SEXUAL PERVERSION

It has been customary in most right wing and racial nationalist organizations to relegate issues such as homosexuality, feminism, and other sexual pervasions to a very low place on the scale of priorities, I have come to the conclusion over the years that this is a mistake. I now feel that any White revolutionary party needs to upgrade the struggle against perversion significantly. For one thing, it is now beginning to appear that organized, militant perversion is a much more prominent part of the enemy's strategic scenario than in years heretofore. In addition, it is now the area in which the enemy is arguably the most vulnerable, thanks to those four little letters that are God's greatest gift to our cause since the Führer Adolf Hitler himself: *A-I-D-S!* Whether or not you regard AIDS as a sign of direct divine intervention or simply a fortuitous accident, the fact remains that it has galvanized White opinion worldwide in a manner that nothing else has done. Of all the enemy's assaults against our religious beliefs, our innate decency, and our sense of order, the worst has always been militant and brazen public faggotry. Dazed and numbed Whites who staggered from work to boob tube to bed and back to work had become programmed to accept virtually anything, but open faggotry was a bit much even for them.

The doubts were always there. *Everything else* the System handed White people, they swallowed. They swallowed integration as long as they could run away from it; they swallowed the fiasco of Vietnam; they swallowed Watergate and the media lynching of an American President; they swallowed the hordes of brown immigrants that Carter deluged us with; they swallowed busing; they swallowed inflation and artificial fuel shortages and massive corruption that marbles our society like fat marbles a steak. But faggotry was just a wee bit too much. No matter how often it was pounded into White America's head that homosexuality wasn't really a perversion but an "alternative lifestyle," it somehow just never sat quite right.

Then, like a bolt from the blue, like the Act of God that it may well be, came AIDS! All of a sudden White America boiled over, broke the chains and restraints. At long last, using AIDS as an excuse, White people could really *say what they felt about faggots!* And from saying and openly admitting what they really feel about queers, it is only a short step to saying what they feel about those other major AIDS carriers, the blacks. Already it's starting to boil over in that area as well. Freedom of speech can be habit forming, and once Whites get used to it they can throw away the AIDS crutch and shout from the rooftops their real views on faggots, niggers, drug addicts, all the garbage we've been forced to wallow in. And who knows? Once Whites get *really* used to speaking their mind, maybe Yehudi himself might come in for a mention or two.

In addition, AIDS is actually doing our work for us far better than any violent revolution could. It is too much to hope that AIDS will kill off all our enemies without us having to lift a finger, but then again ....? Right now there are something like *one hundred and twenty million carriers* in sub-Sahara Africa alone, all of whom will eventually die unless medical science comes up with a cure. What an abundant harvest of kaffirs! More than the entire South African army could wipe out in twenty years. In America the vast majority of AIDS antibody-positives are non-White *or Jewish!* The Jew faggots in New York are paying dearly now for all those dirty weekends down in Haiti. They thought they were getting a bargain, indulging their taste for dark meat more cheaply and certainly more safely than they could in Spanish Harlem. But they brought it to America, it spread to San Francisco, and now all of a sudden in 1987 the powerful homosexual lobby is on the run. A decade-old offensive against the White family in America has been stopped cold. Dead cold.

There is now a growing body of evidence that the hysterical, crazed faggots are trying to take us with them. They are deliberately getting work in restaurants so they can spit in the food; they are deliberately donating their tainted blood to blood banks in the hopes it will escape the Red Cross screening procedures and be transfused into heterosexuals; they are deliberately engaging in heterosexual intercourse in order to spread the disease; they are even raping women on occasion. This has done wonders for their popularity rating in White America, never very high to begin with. At the rate things are going, I freely predict that there are going to be some faggot lynchings at some time in the future. Even if a cure is eventually found—*and no successful cure has yet been found for any virus, including the common cold!* — the AIDS epidemic will eventually drive homosexuality so far back into the closet that it won't dare peep out for another century.

My brothers, the AIDS epidemic is one of our major propaganda weapons. Let us use it to the hilt! Emphasize that there is only one way to avoid AIDS, and that is to *avoid certain types of behavior* and to *avoid the people who engage in that behavior.* And of course, the kind of "life-style" that transmits AIDS is the precise kind of behavior that our enemies engage in. AIDS could have been tailor-made for us! It is possible, of course, that a vaccine will be found not a month after this book is published, in which case this section is already obsolete. But somehow I doubt it. It's been a few thousand years since the Lord struck down Sodom and Gomorrah, but it looks like His patience has finally been exhausted.

There are going to be some Whites who die of AIDS, either through accidental transmission during blood transfusions or grafts, or else because a faggot or druggie has deliberately given it to an unsuspecting person. But then we have always known that we must take some casualties, and a White heterosexual who contracts AIDS either accidentally or through enemy action is just as much a hero and martyr as if he or she was gunned down by Federal troops. I only wish that their deaths might be as quick.

I think I must now address a subject that I have been debating over in my own mind. Should I mention it at all? Ignoring the problem won't make it go away, of course, but then I have to deal with the probability that eventually the enemy will read this book and I believe there are certain internal Movement problems that don't need to be aired anywhere that the enemy might get hold of them.

You will see that I am having a hard time getting to the point. This is probably because I dread getting to the point, which is this: there are some otherwise totally sincere racial nationalists who are also homosexuals, and who through some bizarre perversion of thought as well as body which I cannot begin to comprehend, can evidently see nothing at all incompatible between their genuinely held political and social beliefs and their loathsome personal practices. To say, "Other than the fact that I'm gay I'm a dedicated White revolutionary!" is like saying "Other than that, Mrs, Lincoln, how did you enjoy the play?"

And yet believe it or not, there seems to be some divergence of opinion here within the Movement, especially in Europe. When I went to England during my government-enforced perambulation some years back, I was shocked and horrified at the level of tolerance which I found in the National Front for homosexuality. For some reason the British seem to be even more prone to this vice than other nations, but that doesn't excuse turning the blind eye. (I should also point out that the British National Party, the major British nationalist group at present, takes a strong and sternly correct attitude against perversion and that the "Tommy Atkins" rank and file British nationalist is strongly antipoofter.)

This phenomenon is sufficiently common so that virtually every nationalist of any stripe, with any lengthy experience in the Movement, can tell at least one personal anecdote of the racist homosexual. It is to-tally beyond me why these people cannot understand that what they do puts them beyond the pale of civilized society and human decency. They are actually surprised and upset to learn that they can't join the party or group in question and put forward all manner of absurd and specious arguments, the gist of which is that "sexual preference" is some kind of totally private affair. This is utter hogwash. In the first place, a White revolutionary has no private life. In the second place "sexual preference" in this case affects the whole prime directive guiding our Movement, *the survival of the White race.* There can be no White babies born if the necessary preliminaries don't take place. Indeed, this is precisely why the enemy encourages homosexuality among Whites to begin with.

Let me explain this whole homo thing as best I can. A homosexual is a man or a woman who is deliberately forsaking the natural way of living one's life. A homosexual or lesbian is saying that he or she knows better than the Creator what use his or her body is to be put to. Homosexuality is an attempt to reverse the decision that God's made when the person in question was created. The homosexual is thus a blasphemer in the truest sense. I'm no theologian, but I rather think that the degradation of the human body, which is supposedly cast in God's image, is the only genuine blasphemy. A homosexual not only brazenly places his own inferior judgment against that of the Creator, but he thereby degrades and debases the Creator's own image. About the only thing that can be said at all for faggotry is that it is marginally less wicked than voluntary miscegenation. At least faggots produce no half-breed babies.

I should explain here that I am personally no sexual prude. I don't give a damn what you do in bed so long as you do it with a partner of the same race and the opposite sex. Within those parameters sex is indeed a private affair and no one else's business. But outside those limits it becomes a matter of community concern and public morality. This idea that all sex is a strictly private matter is horse manure; anything involving the perpetuation of the species is a matter for public policy.

Nor should any state of affairs arise wherein a homosexual who has infiltrated the WRP by pretending to be normal, and who then is discovered one way or another, be allowed to remain so long as he "keeps it quiet" and does not forcibly bring his proclivities to the notice of his leaders and his associates. Retaining a fag in the group is like keeping a ticking time bomb in the cellar of your home. One day the whole situation will explode in your party's face. Inversion has an insidious way of coming out, and Murphy's Law dictates that it will come out at precisely the worst time imaginable. Indeed, sometimes the media or the government will know for a long time that there is a homosexual active in such-and-such a group, and either blackmail the individual into informing or hold back the information until the climax of an election campaign or some other crucial time when it can be used against the White organization with devastating effect.

"But so-and-so does so much good for the cause!" may be one objection brought forward. No amount of good that a homo does for the WRP can possibly justify the insane, deadly risk of exposure to the public. It is absolutely essential that the White revolutionary party personify in its leadership and its personnel the ideals for which the revolution is being fought. To be exposed as hypocrites and condoners of perversion would destroy all credibility in the eyes of the White community. *Can all faggots immediately upon detection!*

Feminism is a sexual perversion not only because it generally implies lesbianism but because it literally perverts the natural relationship between men and women. It teaches that men and women are some kind of natural enemies and must exist in a constant state of competition with one another, a perpetual war of one-upmanship. I cannot imagine anything more inimical to the institution of the family and the perpetuation of the White race. Men and women are neither inferior nor superior to each other. They are two halves of a whole and neither is complete without the other. You may recall the famous incident in Paris around the turn of the century, when a well-known women's suffrage leader had been invited to address the national assembly on the subject of votes for women. "Surely you must admit, *monsieurs,*" argued the suffragette at one point in her speech, "that other than mere biology, there is in fact very little difference between men and women?" Thereupon the entire French Chamber of Deputies arose as one man and shouted, *"Vive la difference!"* This is in fact the key to the whole issue. That biological difference is there. It is totally insurmountable. One cannot legislate "equality" between men and women any more than one can pass a law requiring the sun to rise in the west. It just ain't so and no amount of Congressional fiat can *make* it so.

I read about bizarre scientific experiments carried out by ultra-left, ultra-liberal "foundations" and laboratories (tax funded, of course), aimed at finding ways for men to have babies; ways for actual test tube creations of human life without any sexual act at all between man and woman; new artificial insemination techniques designed to impregnate lesbians without forcing them to soil their dumpy bodies with male contact; genetic diddling around with the X and Y chromosomes so that said lesbos can ensure girl children only from the pipette; techniques for injecting male children at birth with female hormones and surgically altering their glands to ensure they grow up hermaphroditic and thus pose no threat to women from their "male aggression" and "phallic extroversion." I read some of the more extreme feminist literature demanding that women be given the right to kill, to practice infanticide and "retroactive abortion" if their children interfere with their "personal development;" to kill any man who offends them and get away with it on a plea of "gender defense;" to remove all legal protection whatsoever from any man accused of rape and allow him to be imprisoned solely on the woman's say-so without corroborating evidence.

I read of women troops to be used in combat. I see bull dykes and little slips of girls tooling around in police cars, wearing men's uniforms and pretending to be cops; some of the silly bimbi can barely carry the weight of their equipment belt, gun and nightstick. I read of suspects shot down without reason because the female cop just wasn't physically big enough to command respect or deal with an aggressive drunk forcefully, so she had to pull her gun and murder some working man. Any normal male cop would have simply tossed him in the back of the squad car and taken him down to the tank to sober up, but ZOG decreed that he must die in the name of idiot social experimentation. I read of female cops panicking during violent situations and shooting themselves or their partners in error.

At the place where I am currently employed (until one of the affirmative action commissar-esses gets hold of a copy of this book), the few males on the floor walk in constant dread of a sexual harassment charge from one of their female co-workers. I have seen this used on several occasions in order to silence criticism of female incompetence and stupidity in their assigned work. (I should also point out that a lot of these women are negresses, and that among the White women there are a few competent exceptions.) All throughout American commerce and industry the horror stories are starting to emerge now, accounts of blackmail, intrigue, false accusations; corporate drumhead courts-martial for "sexism" or alleged sexual harassment which destroy men's careers after years of hard work; "aggressive affirmative action programs" which amount to Soviet style purges of White men in order to make way for Yuppie Barbie dolls; homosexual and/or lesbian cabals in top management with their own hidden agenda; female executives who sexually harass and humiliate their male subordinates. In some companies Big Sister is definitely watching; it is almost like living during the Salem witchcraft panic when any hysterical girl could point a finger and get someone hanged.

I read of attempts to organize women as a bloc vote similar to that of the niggers and spics, for which politicians must negotiate with the bull dyke leaders of NOW and other such bodies. Despite the fact that they were resoundingly defeated on the ERA, militant feminists are plotting another revival of that most sinister of attempts to tamper with the Constitution. "Marital rape" laws are being pushed strongly in order to give wives the power of life or death over their husbands, a weapon of constant blackmail and intimidation which, if enforced, would quite probably destroy marriage as an institution. (As it is no doubt intended to do.) The ongoing mass murder of abortion continues unchecked, a topic I do not intend to address because it is beyond the power of my feeble vocabulary to encompass such a blasphemy against all the universe. All I can say is that if there is a hell, the people responsible for this butchery will burn in agony for untold aeons, and they will deserve every second of it.

Half of all White marriages end in divorce. 25% of all young White men and women of marriageable age live alone. A whole generation of White children are growing up as "latch-key kids," dumped in a day care center or a school every morning before Mommy and Daddy or the single parent of the household goes to work, coming home to an empty house and the boob tube, sometimes with a TV dinner sitting in the oven. More than any nigger gun or knife, more than any needle of heroin or line of coke, more than any perversion of thought practiced by the Jews upon our minds, this so-called "liberation" of women is destroying us.

This is sheer lunatic insanity. IT MUST BE STOPPED! THIS EVIL SYSTEM MUST BE DESTROYED!

We have to stop trying to fight this thing with words and start fighting it with deeds. Can you imagine what this country, what this world is going to be like fifty years from now if these people aren't stopped?

When I was a child I had a benefit so precious, so important, so vital in my development that I cannot imagine what it would have been like without it. *My mother was always home.* When I needed something, when I was hungry or had fallen down and hurt myself or when I had a question, she was *there.* How many White American children nowadays have this precious birthright, a full-time live-in mother? How many more White children now see their mothers only briefly at the end of a hard working day? How many are growing up neglected, poorly fed, starved of affection in some mass herd of children at a day care center where the staff puts on little plays showing the boy dolls kissing other boy dolls and the girl dolls kissing other girl dolls, and where the kids are divided into "play groups" with burr-head piccaninnies as the appointed leaders?

I am absolutely convinced that the economic incompetence which has forced huge numbers of women onto the labor market is part of an overall hidden agenda on the part of our rulers to undermine the family and turn White people into mere units of productive labor to keep some soulless Judaic machine going. It is the common complaint that nowadays a family cannot survive without both husband and wife working. This is horse hockey. Presuming the husband has a job paying middling fair above minimum wage, it is perfectly possible for the wife to stay at home and raise the children, What is *not* possible is to maintain the materialistic American lifestyle on the husband's salary alone.

To start with, who needs that goddamned television? Throw it on the scrap heap and let your kids play outside or read books! Who says you need a new car every year? Learn rudimentary auto mechanics and keep your old one running. Make a long-term investment in a good tape and stereo system and turn your children on to music instead of junk cartoons and cheap, overpriced plastic toys. Better yet, learn to play instruments yourself and teach your children. My own experience is that kids have more fun with simple toys like blocks or erector sets that can satisfy their simultaneous natural urges both to create and to destroy.

Who needs RVs, boats, videos, all that tinsel consumer crap? Who needs Yuppie dinners of nachos and quiche that cost $25 a meal? Feed your family simple home cooking using the basics of meat, potatoes, and vegetables. Who needs a beach home that you'll use maybe five or six weekends in the summer? Learn to practice economy. Insulate your home, air-condition it one room at the time and only when the heat becomes unbearable, use a wood-burning stove in the winter. You can get by on Daddy's income alone if you try, and your children won't grow up to be sullen, introspective neurotics or mindless boob-tubular zombies.

The making of a home and the rearing of a family is the most vital function that exists in ours or any other society. It is also something that only a woman can do. I can sit here and tap out fifty books like this one, ranting and raving about the evils of society and what needs to be done, but even if every word I write here is taken to heart and we have the revolution tomorrow, the whole primary purpose of it all is to create a sane, safe, stable environment for the woman who is the central personage in our world, the mother and homemaker. No matter what brilliant heights of verbose rhetoric I attain, no matter how many Whites I will hopefully inspire to arise from their hindquarters and take action, no matter what success I may meet, I still can't have a baby and bring another White life into the world. That is a miracle only our sisters can perform, the same sisters whose minds and hearts are being corrupted by feminist lies and whose bodies are being stolen from us by dykes and mud-men because we White men are too goddamned spineless and too bloody lazy to lift a finger to stop it.

Lose our women, my brothers, and we lose everything. All our dedication, all our courage on the field of battle, all our planning and our hard work will be for nothing if we lose the heart and soul of our ladies. And if we let them go without a fight, then history and manifest destiny will have judged us and found us unworthy, and we will deserve extinction.

XII.
TO THOSE WHO SHALL COME AFTER

This final chapter is directed towards a moment in your lives and your political careers which will inevitably come. I refer to the moment when you are just about ready to fold up and call it quits. It is a moment which happens to all of us at some time or other. Yuppies call it "burnout;" I used to call it "the eighteenth month crisis" because I noticed it generally hit people first about a year and a half after they got involved.

Let me articulate for you the feelings you will have, the despair you will be undergoing. I know how because I have undergone it myself on more than one occasion and even more so because I have heard it so often from other comrades. Why hasn't there been any visible progress? Are we doing something wrong? We've got to change this, change that, change the other thing. We've got to change our party name, change our position on something else, change our symbol, change our tactics. Why, why, oh *why* won't they *listen* to us? Why won't they *wake up?* Why can't we get any kind of fair shake or unbiased treatment from the media? We've got to tone things down, become "respectable" so we won't be constantly slandered and abused in the press and on TV. Why won't the White people wake up and listen to us? Why won't they help? Can't they see we're doing this for *them?* Oh, they're just so damnably, utterly *stupid*! Why can't they understand? Why *won't* they understand? They're greedy and lazy and selfish and brainless nitwits, that's why! Well, to hell with them! They're not worth having! None of this is worth doing because White people are useless, worthless jackasses! Let them die! Let the Jews have it all and then see if they can control the niggers and spics! I'm dropping out! I'm gonna move way, way out into the woods someplace and wait for the Balloon to go up!

Or words to that effect, I've heard it all more times than I care to remember, in more ways than I can count, in dozens of different variations. Sometimes the people involved do quit and never return. Sometimes they drop out for a while and come back when their psychic batteries are re-charged. Sometimes they just plain fall to pieces. I have seen the frustration and despair and rage that this struggle engenders destroy people from within, driving them to alcoholism, suicide, bizarre self-destructive behavior. A few have even deliberately and consciously defected to the enemy, "finding Jesus" and going on the talk show circuit telling all about how I was a terrible racist but now the love of Jesus is in me and I'm married to a lovely Mexican woman and we're adopting a Third World child and blah, blah, blah. For this, the Jews contemptuously throw a handful of green paper at the traitor's feet, and eventually the interracial marriage breaks up and the traitor goes on drugs or booze and becomes too disgusting even for the media to touch.

Or, like Jim Harris, the defector wakes up one morning and realizes what he has done. (Harris is not this man's real name, since his family still live in North Carolina and I don't want to cause them any more pain than they have already been through.) His story, though, is tragic. Harris took burnout beyond the pale: he ended by shacking up with a negress. One day he appears to have awakened and suddenly the enormity of his betrayal struck him like the weight of a mountain. He arose from the odoriferous arms of his dusky Sheba, put on a Swastika armband that he still had from the old days, left a brief yet pithy note behind him telling his bubble-lipped dulcinea just what he thought of her, and then loaded up his rifle and walked down to a local nigger church picnic for some target practice. When the SWAT team finally killed him, he had taken some Ubangis with him; he went down with his weapon firing. Like the Thane of Cawdor in *Macbeth,* nothing in his life so became him as his manner of leaving it.

Let me make it clear that I do not approve of the choice James Harris made, and I truly wish that he had made another, if only because that sort of thing was lousy publicity for the party. But I think I can understand why he chose as he did. He had once attempted the greatest of all services to humanity, a duty so sublime that like all of us he craved it as an addict craves his drug. And yet there came a bad patch, and rather than weathering it, he threw in the towel. More than that, he had deliberately trampled upon his former vocation, defiling his body with that of an animal. How could he ever come back to us after that? There was no way. His death in a blaze of enemy gunfire was his way of saying to us and to posterity, "I do truly repent. Take my life in penance, and know that I died with my heart and my soul cleansed of the filth."

Someday we will have some kind of national cemetery or memorial for our brothers and sisters who have died in the cause. When that day comes, I think that if I have anything to say about it, I could see my way to allowing Jim's name a place in the inscription and his remains a rest-ing place in the hallowed ground. Glory is a strange commodity and it crops up in strange places.

This case is an extreme example of what White racial burnout can do, but it's a first class bummer in any case. Each of you is going to have to face it, and each of you is going to have to come to terms with it and defeat it — or not — as best you can. I'll close this book with a final piece of advice, as briefly as I can put it.

We do what we do not because we have any immediate hope of victory, we do not do it in order to produce tangible, immediately visible results, because this is impossible. We must accept from the very beginning that we will work and fight and struggle for years in almost total isolation, in the dark, very seldom seeing any of the big picture and even less frequently observing any progress. The enemy is just too big and strong and we are too small and weak.

We must never allow ourselves the luxury of hope. We are the dead. It is our children who will live, and their children after them, in the glorious, safe, joyous White Aryan future we will create for them. We will participate in that future, our bodies as motes of dust and grains of sand, our souls (so I believe) in the bodies of our descendants who will reward us in their happy, productive, and creative lives for the darkness and the suffering that we now undergo in these waning years of this bloody and hideous century.

We do what we do for one reason only: *because it is right.* We do it because our Creator commands us through our thoughts, our soul, our genetic instincts, to follow His path and work His will. We fight against the forces of darkness because that's our bag, baby, Battling evil is what us White folks do on this earth. I mean, like, it's our thing. Dig it?

"This destiny does not tire, nor can it be broken, and its mantle of strength descends upon those in its service." wrote the author of *Imperium.* When your moment of crisis comes, search within yourself. If you are willing to make the necessary effort of will, then you will find the strength that you need to carry on.

Good luck, my brothers and sisters. And good hunting.

EPILOGUE

"You will know, I am sure, that strength and weapons alone do not always prevail in battle. When an army is stronger in soul, then their enemies cannot withstand them."

— Xenophon

Four hundred years before Christ, a Persian prince named Cyrus plotted to overthrow his brother Artaxerxes and thus become Great King of all Persia. For this he needed an army, but the locals were a sorry lot, and so he turned to the Greek cities of Asia Minor and the northern plains of Thrace and Macedonia, renowned for breeding the tall, blond soldiers called hoplites, masters of the bow and spear and sword. With only a few of these disciplined, formidable Greek warriors in bronze armor, Cyrus was confident he could defeat his brother's rag-bag Asiatic tribesmen.

Cyrus retained a renegade Spartan commander named Clearchus to recruit a mercenary army with which to overthrow the Persian monarch. Clearchus is referred to in the chronicles of the time as a severe disciplinarian "of grim feature and harsh voice;" indeed, he must have been a pretty rough character to get run out of Sparta, since the Spartans weren't exactly sweetness and light themselves. But Clearchus had that indispensable quality, a reputation for victory, and Greek warriors rushed to join him. I imagine they were the usual assortment of men who have served in every army of our mighty race — freebooters, young men seeking strange sights and new knowledge, ne'er-do-wells looking for a fast buck, second sons seeking their fortunes, farmers seeking land, henpecked husbands seeking the relative peace and quiet of war, drifters with nothing better to do, violent men who loved combat for its own sake, men seeking for whatever reason to efface their past, professional soldiers who fought because that was what they did in life. Their kind won us the whole world, using spear and sword and flintlock musket and Navy Colt. We have repaid them by throwing that world away and spitting on their graves. At any rate, Cyrus soon had his army.

In the old accounts they are generally called the Ten Thousand Adventurers.

They shouldered their spears and they marched out of the Greek city of Sardis in May of 401 B.C. After a long and complicated campaign they finally came up against Artaxerxes and the main Persian army in September, near a village just outside Babylon called Cunaxa. The Greeks attacked ferociously and smashed the Persian host to bits, but at the last minute disaster struck. The Persian prince Cyrus made a foolish personal attack against the royal palace guard in an attempt to personally slay his brother, and for his trouble he ended up getting hacked to pieces. On his death, the Persian allies of the invading rebel force threw down their weapons and ran. The Ten Thousand now found themselves confronting a revitalized Persian army all alone, at least 100,000 Asiatic spearmen, slingers, archers, swordsmen, chariots, cavalry, and war elephants.

It was here that Clearchus made a fatal mistake. Believing an offer of truce from Artaxerxes, he rode forward with his main generals and captains to negotiate a compromise settlement. With truly Semitic treachery, the Persians seized them and murdered them as they rode in unarmed.

The Ten Thousand were now in a very bad way. They were 1,500 miles from the nearest Greek city, Trapezus on the Euxine Sea. They had no food, very little water, their baggage train had been destroyed by the Persians, they had no guides or experienced officers left, they were exhausted from fighting a long battle, and they were about to be overrun by 100,000 wogs. They met on a hill near Cunaxa and elected as their new general a young Athenian nobleman named Xenophon. Xenophon was not a professional soldier but a scholar and a poet, a pupil of Socrates, and he had enlisted in the expedition as a private in order to write a book about it.

Nonetheless, the Greeks had made the right choice, because Xenophon took command as if born to it. The Persians attacked, but Xenophon counterattacked and captured the Great King's own baggage train and all his supplies, a welcome development for the hungry Greeks. He feinted an attack against Babylon itself and managed to so confuse the Persians that the Ten Thousand were able to break contact and escape. Wisely, Artaxerxes did not follow, but sent his satrap Tissaphernes in pursuit.

The epic retreat that followed is one of the greatest stories of endurance, fortitude, brilliant generalship, and Aryan courage that graces the annals of our mighty race. At Trapezus were ships that would return them to Greece, but in between lay 1,500 miles of desert, impassable rivers, barren mountains, hostile tribesmen, Persian armies, and bad weather. Yet the Ten Thousand marched on. They fought half a dozen battles and eventually defeated Tissaphernes decisively. They cut their way out of countless ambushes. They laid siege to cities and exacted food and tribute from them. Xenophon overcame mutinies, conspiracies, assassination attempts, disease, starvation, and enemy attacks. At every mountain pass and village he left dead comrades, but the remaining mercenaries marched on.

Finally, in January of 400 B.C., the Greeks wearily climbed a mountain. The ancient chronicle goes on, "And when the van reached the summit a great cry arose. When Xenophon and the rear heard it, they thought an enemy was attacking in the front ..and galloped forward with their cavalry. When they drew near, Xenophon heard what the cry was — *'The sea! The sea!'* " They had made it. Five days later they entered the Greek city and thence dispersed to their homes.

My brothers, my sisters, imagine it! After all those weary marches, all those deaths, all that treachery, all that fear and anguish, imagine what it must have been like to hear that shout!

"The sea! The sea!"

They were home. They made it. We'll make it too, my beloved brothers and sisters. I promise it. I swear it. Maybe not you and I as individuals, no. That I can't promise. But someday, somewhere, that cry will arise from White throats parched with thirst and dry of hope.

"The sea! The sea!"

We may not hear it. But I think our children will, and if not them, then certainly our grandchildren. For deep down inside, our spears are as sharp and our courage as great as that of the Ten Thousand. We left our Cunaxa in 1945. It will take us longer than it did Xenophon and his men, to be sure — but one day we, too, shall climb the last mountain and see the sea.

When he returned home, Xenophon wrote his book about his experiences, the things he had seen, the battles he had fought, the people he had met. He entitled this book *Anabasis.* Most Greek scholars today translate this as "The March Up Country."

www.ingramcontent.com/pod-product-compliance
Lightning Source LLC
Chambersburg PA
CBHW021342290326
41933CB00037B/338

* 9 7 8 1 5 9 3 6 4 0 0 9 5 *